HELLO

BENTO DELIGHTS

adorable + stylish lunches on the go

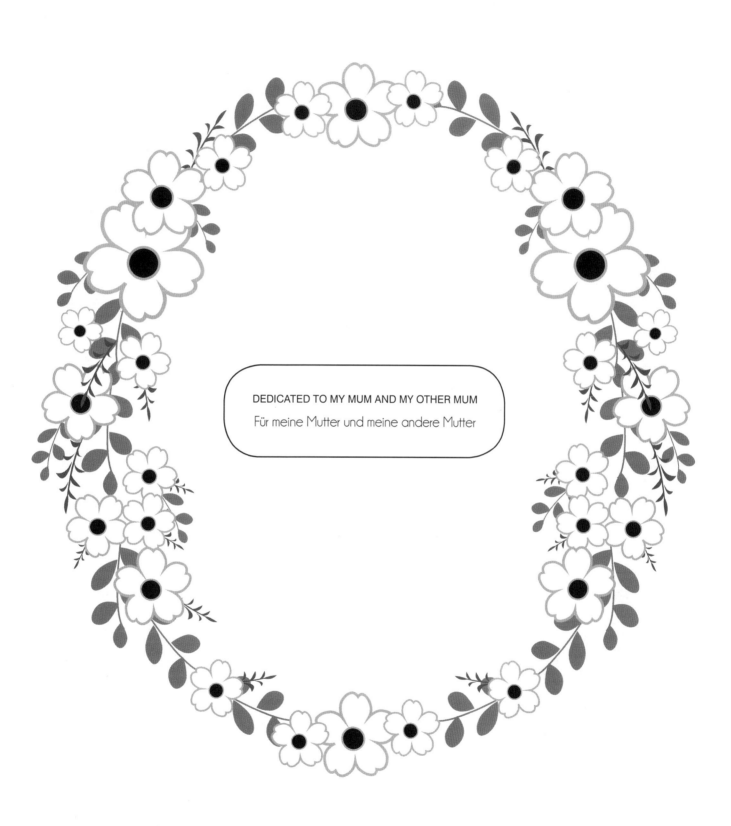

DEDICATED TO MY MUM AND MY OTHER MUM

Für meine Mutter und meine andere Mutter

TABLE OF CONTENTS

INTRODUCTION

Bento or *obento* is the Japanese word for compact and portable meal packed in a box, which is usually eaten at lunch. My love for Japanese bento boxes began several years ago, when pictures of adorable bento lunches started popping up in Japanese manga I used to love reading while growing up. However, I did not start making bento myself until February 2011. I love preparing elaborate character bento, generally known as *charaben* or *kyaraben*, since I enjoy the creative process involved in making cute characters or intricate patterns out of food. But I also take great pleasure in preparing more simple, yet elegant traditional bento meals.

The recipes in this cookbook focus on modern Asian cuisine – especially Japanese, Korean and Chinese. Most of the dishes can be prepared quickly, but there are a few exceptions which need longer time to put together. However, these are usually good for freezing or can be stored in the fridge for some time. The bento menus and designs included in this book only serve as a guide and inspirations for people who want to try making more decorative bento meals at home. You are certainly free to change the ingredients, condiments, or anything else to suit your needs – after all it is your lunch!

It is important to note that this book is not written with the intention to give parents fun lunch ideas for kids who are picky eaters. The Character Bento section can certainly help parents to get some basic ideas on how to make edible cute characters. However, you will notice that a lot of the recipes are more geared towards older audience and people interested in Japanese or modern Asian cuisine in general. If you are new to bento, I recommend you to check out the glossary before you start browing the recipes, to familiarise yourself with some possible novel terms and ingredients used repeatedly in this book.

For more bento inspirations and recipes, please visit my food blog, cookinggallery.blogspot.com, which started off as a hobby in mid 2009. The support I have received from my blog readers so far have been tremendous, and without their encouragements, well wishes and kind support, this book would have never been written in the first place.

This cookbook is authored and designed solely by me and all of the bento photos were photographed by yours truly with my beloved Canon pocket camera. I also illustrated all of the graphics and patterns displayed in this book. Writing this book has been a challenging, albeit interesting journey. I hope this cookbook could be a source of inspiration for everyone who is new to bento making, or just anyone who is interested to give their lunch a little bling.

BENTO BASICS

I am absolutely no bento expert, but I like to cook and I have always found aesthetically arranged foods very appealing. Ever since I started blogging about bento, I have received numerous e-mails from people all over the world asking me how to pack bento boxes properly and how long it normally takes me to prepare those bento boxes shown in my blog. From reading these e-mails and various comments I see online about bento lunches, I get the impression that a lot of people seem to regard packing bento as something too unattainable and exotic, when in fact the opposite is true.

I suppose that when people think of bento boxes, they directly associate the word *bento* with super stylised food made by Japanese super mums, or with those delicate and exclusive bento boxes they see in expensive Japanese restaurants. However, this is just a misconception. Bento is simply the Western equivalent of a packed lunch. It doesn't have to be decorated and when you pack a regular BLT sandwich in a lunch container, it is also considered a bento.

This cookbook is divided into two main sections: Character Bento and Traditional Bento. Below you will find more information about what exactly these two types of bento are, and some packing tips that might come in handy when you want to start making your own bento lunch.

CHARACTER BENTO

More commonly known as *charaben* or *kyaraben*, character bento refers to an intricately arranged bento box, which includes food that have been made to resemble characters from popular media, people, animals, plants and other items from nature. This trend started in Japan, possibly in mid 1990s, and was initially intended as a method to motivate children to eat healthier. Nowadays, *charaben* is pretty common in Japan and is slowly gaining attention worldwide due to the internet and online social media. I sometimes like to make *charaben*, and a few years ago I did make *charaben* regularly. It is certainly not everyone's cup of tea and it might appeal more to children than adults. Nonetheless I enjoy making *charaben*. I consider it an art form with the bento box as my canvas – I am sure other *charaben* enthusiasts and creatives out there know what I am talking about!

However, I am aware that *charaben* can be quite time consuming to make, especially if the design is rather complex. Looking at our modern hectic lifestyle, making *charaben* on a daily basis is possible, but not very practical – and I suppose you have to like what you do, or you will find it totally meaningless in the long run. I have especially chosen to include 15 character bentos with rather simple but still adorable designs in this book. They are not too difficult to execute and with good planning, they are even suitable for everyday bento!

TRADITIONAL BENTO

Traditional bento is a term which I use loosely in this book to describe simple and practical packed lunches. It is much less time-consuming to assemble compared to *charaben*, and much more realistic to prepare on a daily basis – basically the opposite of *charaben*, but this doesn't mean that you are not supposed to decorate this type of bento at all. You certainly can, but I usually use minimal effort and simply add cute vegetable cutouts to make my traditional bento appear more fancy.

PACKING TIPS

Incorporate a variety of food items

Rather than packing one big portion of food, try to include small portions of different food items to add textures and flavours, and to make your bento instantly more visually appealing. I don't follow any rules on what to put in my bento box. Generally, I just pack what I like to eat, even though I always incorporate vegetables and fruit in my bento, not just for the health benefits, but also because they make my bento looks so happy and colourful!

Design = Taste = Nutrition

Ideally, a bento should be aesthetically pleasing to the eye and equally tasty and nutritious. Balanced nutrition is certainly important, but I am not too fussy about it. However, I think that beautifully presented bento should definitely be tasty. Do not override taste just for the sake of a beautiful design!

Plan Ahead + Use Leftovers

Planning ahead and stocking up on homemade and store-bought foods are essential for a speedy bento making. I like to make a big batch of bento friendly foods, such as Chinese dumplings and chicken nuggets, and freeze them for later use. Using leftovers for your bento is also a good trick to reduce your preparation time. After all, who wants to whip up three or more different variety of foods early in the morning?

Prepare the Night Before

If you are planning to make *charaben*, cut out nori facial details or any other decorative elements the night before to save time in the morning. Even if you just want to pack a simple, traditional bento, pre-washing and pre-cutting vegetables and fruit in advance, and making sure that your bento box and other equipments are all set and ready to go, is another great way to cut down your bento preparation time in the morning.

Let Cool + Fill Any Gaps

Cool completely before closing the lid, to avoid food from spoiling. Make sure you fill the bento box fully and fill any gaps with bento fillers such as broccoli florets, cherry tomatoes or mini sauce containers. Pack tightly to make sure that the food items do not move around during transportation.

Secure Decorative Elements

Making sure that decorative elements in your bento box stay intact during transportation could also be challenging. Mayonnaise is often used as edible glue to attach nori details. You can also use other possible edible glue such as cream cheese or ketchup. Use little pieces of uncooked spaghetti noodle to secure tiny vegetable cutouts or other food items that need to stay in place.

BENTO BOXES + TOOLS + ACCESSORIES

There are endless varieties of bento boxes and fun tools available to help you make creative bento lunches. However, you don't actually need specialised equipment to start making your own bento box meals! In fact, the first time I started to make my own bento lunch, I didn't own any fancy bento supplies but one lunch container. I used ordinary kitchen items such as plastic wrap, paring knife and small kitchen scissors to make my first character bento - and it turned out pretty adorable!

Tools and accessories that are designed specifically for bento making are certainly convenient and can be a great time saver, but they are not essential, especially if your main focus is to prepare simple, traditional bento. However, if what you are striving for is to make elaborate bento meals, I suggest to invest in tiny cutters and nori punches that are made especially to decorate quail eggs. In essence, spend your money on bento tools and accessories which can help you create something which is otherwise too time consuming to make yourself.

MY ESSENTIAL BENTO TOOLS

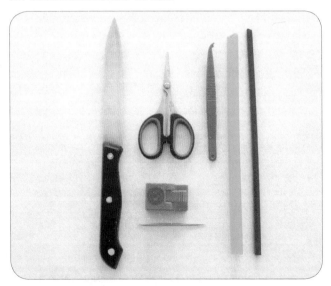

Paring knife

A good sharp paring knife is very valuable. You can use it to cut fruits, vegetables and other food items into interesting shapes. Let your imagination run wild and even a humble kitchen knife could transform your bento into something more intriguing!

Scissors

I usually use micro-tip scissors to cut nori seaweed into different shapes. If you don't have any nori punches, micro-tip scissors can come in very handy. They are nevertheless not a must. Small hobby scissors will do just fine too.

Tweezers

Tweezers are good for placing tiny decorative elements onto food items. I usually use tweezers to apply seaweed eyes or smiles onto characters' faces. Toothpicks can also do a similar job, but tweezers give you better hand control.

Straws

Drinking straws are great for cutting out round shapes and they are a cheaper alternative to round bento cutters and decorating tips. Collect different sizes of straws and they would be very useful for your future *charaben* escapades.

Toothpicks

Toothpicks can be used to cut cheese into shapes. They are also great for dabbing ketchup onto edible characters' faces to make rosy cheeks, and they are useful for securing loose foods too!

Mini Nori Punches

The nori punches I can't live without are the ones which are specifically designed to decorate quail eggs. They produce super tiny and very fine nori cutouts that are almost impossible to recreate just with the help of micro tip scissors. These types of nori punches are ideal for decorating quail eggs, mini bocconcini, cherry tomatoes and other small food items.

> ### HYGIENE
>
> When making bento, especially character bento, use utensils such as tweezers, toothpicks and chopsticks to arrange food items. I try not to touch the foods too much, when decorating my bento, because I don't find food items that have been touched repeatedly with bare hands very appetising – I don't think that it's very hygienic either!
>
> Please make sure to only use your bento equipment, tools and accessories strictly for kitchen use. I shuddered when I once heard that somebody use her eyebrow plucker as kitchen tweezers, and this is no joke!

BENTO BOXES available on the market range from plastic bento boxes, stainless steel to the more traditional and elegant wooden bento boxes. These boxes are often beautiful to look at and fun to collect, but they are not a necessity. When shopping for a bento box, look for a sturdy box that seals well. You can start with a regular zip lock or Tupperware container. If you like to keep your lunch warm, use a thermal lunch jar, which can easily be bought online. Most bento boxes nowadays are also microwave and dishwasher safe, which is a plus!

If you adore wooden bento boxes like me, you have to keep in mind that even though they are indeed very lovely, they tend to be rather pricey and are not microwave and dishwasher safe, and you need to take a little extra care when washing these little beauties by hand. I usually wash my wooden boxes with warm water and mild detergent. Don't forget to wipe them dry after washing. If you take care of them well, they will last for a very very long time!

NORI PUNCHES are a wonderful time saver. Instead of cutting out funky shapes with scissors, nori punches do the job for you within seconds. You can also use regular paper punches found at craft or stationary stores, they basically do the same job!

SAUCE CONTAINERS are used to hold condiments such as mayonnaise, soy sauce, ketchup and salad dressing. Containers with a wide cap are good for thicker sauces, while mini sauce bottles are for liquid condiments.

CUTTERS are excellent for bento making. Cookie cutters, vegetable cutters and even fondant cutters are great choices. Use metal cutters to cut raw vegetables and plastic ones to cut softer foods.

MINI FOOD CUPS function as food separator. I personally like silicone cups best, as they are re-useable and flexible, so they can fit in odd spaces. Food cups made of plastic and baking cups made of paper or aluminium work just as well. The choice is yours, you have to work out yourself which type of food cups works best for you.

FOOD DIVIDERS or *baran* in Japanese, have a similar use to food cups. They keep foods with incompatible flavours separated. A lot of charaben lovers like to use *baran* simply for decorative purposes. I myself prefer to use lettuce or other vegetables such as broccoli florets and cucumbers to segregate foods.

DECORATIVE FOOD PICKS are not just super cute, they are practical too. You can use them as mini forks or for skewering foods together. They make great decorative elements to your bento meals due to their vibrant colours and eye catching designs.

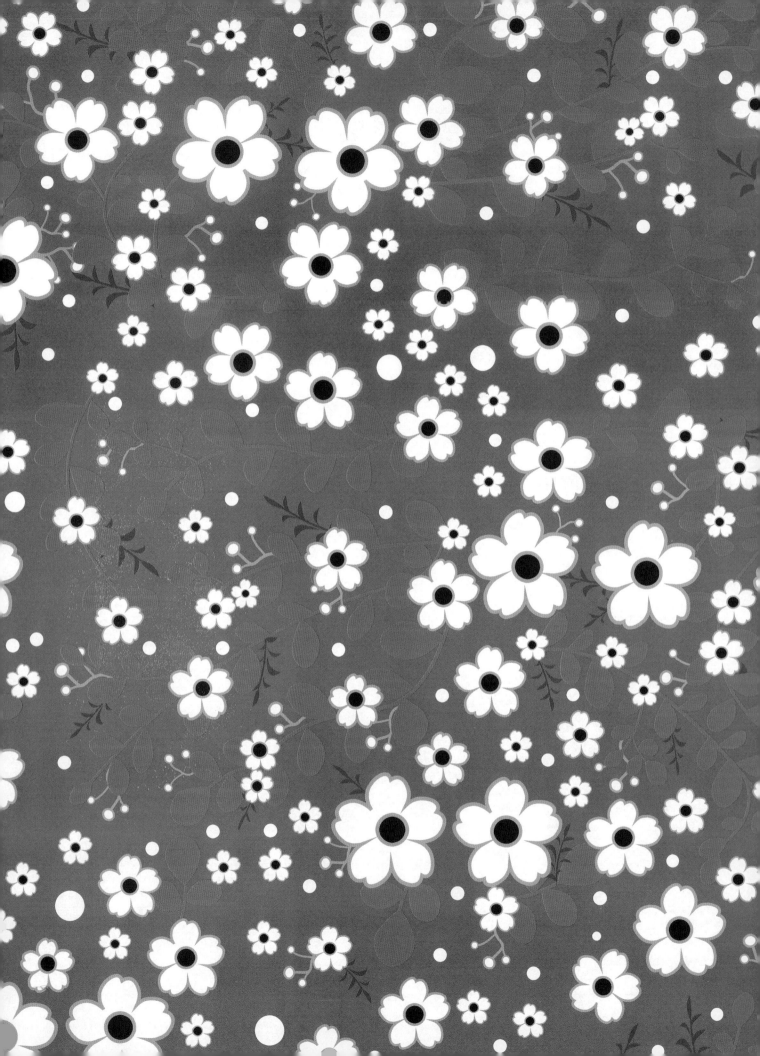

CHARACTER BENTO

18
WHITE
KOALA BENTO

20
SMILING
PANDA BENTO

22
BLACK
KITTY BENTO

24
BABYBEL
CHICK BENTO

26
CHEEKY
PIGLET BENTO

28
ELMO
BENTO

30
MINI FROG + CHICK
SANDWICH BENTO

32
PINK
CHICK BENTO

34
THREE
LITTLE PIGS BENTO

36
BROWN BEAR BURGER
PICNIC BENTO

38
CHEERFUL
MONKEY BENTO

40
FRIENDLY
POLAR BEAR BENTO

42
FLUFFY BEAR
ONIGIRI BENTO

44
BASHFUL
BUNNY BENTO

46
FUNKY
PENGUIN BENTO

48
LOVELY
LION BENTO

WHITE KOALA BENTO

I think that koala is one of the cutest animals on earth! Have you ever seen pure white koalas? They are extremely rare, but you can also have your own white koala bears by making them out of mini bocconcini – fresh mozzarella balls about the size of cherry tomatoes. They are very delicate yet refreshing and delightfully creamy. Definitely my favourite cheese!

BOCCONCINI KOALAS
MAKES 1

2 mini bocconcini (1 for the head, 1 for the ears)
1 small piece nori seaweed
1 pickled black olive
1 uncooked spaghetti noodle

EQUIPMENT

small kitchen knife
nori punch
small round cutter
toothpick

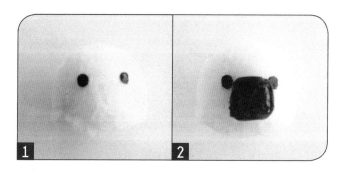

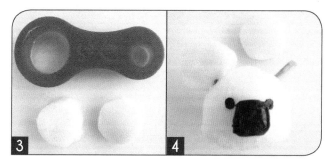

TIP

Use the toothpick to dab some ketchup on the koala's cheeks. If you cannot find fresh bocconcini, substitute with hard-boiled quail eggs or white coloured fish balls, which are usually available at most Asian grocery stores.

1. Use the nori punch to cut two black dots out of nori for the eyes. Place them on one of the bocconcini balls.

2. Use the knife to cut a square-shaped nose out of a piece of black olive.

3. Cut the remaining bocconcini into ½ cm thick slices. Punch two small circles out of the bocconcini slices to make the ears.

4. Attach the ears to the little koala's head and secure them with two small pieces of uncooked spaghetti noodle.

SMILING PANDA BENTO

These smiling cheese pandas are adorable and pretty simple to make, especially if you own a panda nori punch and a teddy bear cutter. But do not fret if you don't, you can always use a toothpick to manually cut the teddy bear shape out of cheese and little micro-tip scissors to cut out the nori faces. Look at the "Cheerful Monkey Bento" tutorial on page 38 as an example.

CHEESE PANDAS
MAKES 2

| 1 slice goat cheese (or other light-coloured cheese) |
| 1 piece nori seaweed |
| 1 slice red radish |
| 1 tsp ketchup |

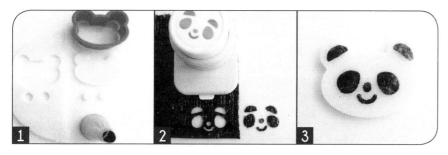

1   Use a teddy bear cutter to cut the panda's head out of cheese, and use a round decorating tip to punch out the paws.

2   Use a panda nori punch to cut the ears, eyes, nose and smile out of nori seaweed.

3   Attach the nori face details to the cheese panda.

4   Top each of the two little cheese paws with four dots punched out of nori.

5   Cut a heart shape out of a slice of radish.

6   Dab on rosy ketchup cheeks with a toothpick

CONTENTS

EQUIPMENT

teddy bear cutter

mini heart cutter

nori punches

round decorating tip

TIP

Use a thin drinking straw to punch out the paws, if you don't have a round decorating tip.

I consider this character bento one of the easiest and quickest to make, providing that you have some leftover fried rice and tamagoyaki from the night before. Add a ham ribbon by placing two small ham rolls topped with a piece of blanched pea under the kitty's head. This bento is not just cute, it's delicious too!

BLACK KITTY BENTO

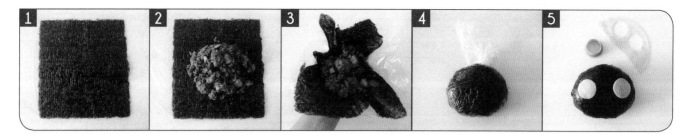

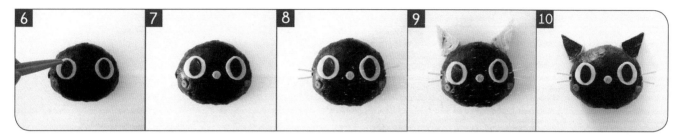

CONTENTS

Black Kitty Onigiri

Mashed Purple Potato Salad – 87

Vegetarian Pasta Salad – 86

Boiled Edamame Beans

Fruit

BLACK KITTY ONIGIRI

MAKES 4

8 – 10 Tbsp seafood fried rice – 85

1 sheet nori seaweed (18 x 20 cm)

2 slices tamagoyaki – 97

1 slice smoked turkey

¼ slice smoked ham

1 thinly sliced carrot coin, blanched

1 uncooked spaghetti noodle

EQUIPMENT

round cutter

thin drinking straw

small scissors

small kitchen knife

1 sheet plastic wrap

1 Place a sheet of nori seaweed on top of a plastic wrap.

2 Put 8 – 10 tablespoons seafood fried rice (or any other type of fried rice) in the middle of the nori seaweed.

3 Gather and wrap the nori seaweed around the rice.

4 Twist the plastic wrap to make sure that the nori seaweed fully seals the rice ball, while shaping it into an oval.

5 Use the round cutter to cut two circles out of smoked turkey for the eyes.

6 Place two nori eyes on top of the smoked turkey eyes.

7 Use the thin drinking straw to cut out one ham nose and rosy carrot cheeks.

8 Add the whiskers by sticking little pieces of spaghetti into the rice ball.

9 To make the ears, cut the tamagoyaki slices into triangles. Break 2 small pieces of spaghetti noodle and poke them through the tamagoyaki ears into the cat's head.

10 Optional Step: To make the ears black, cut two triangles out of nori and place them on top of the tamagoyaki ears.

BABYBEL CHICK BENTO

This would be a great Easter bento! What could have been easier than to make a lovable, edible chick out of yellow Babybel cheese? Give this a shot! It's not as intimidating as it seems!

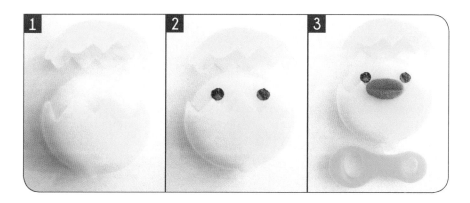

EQUIPMENT

paring knife

assortment of cutters

nori punch, or scissors

TIP

Use mayonnaise as glue to attach the nori eyes, and stick small pieces of uncooked spaghetti through the potato flower, carrot beak and carrot feet into the Babybel cheese, to make sure that everything stays in place.

BABYBEL CHICKS
MAKES 2

2 yellow Babybel cheese

1 small piece nori seaweed

1 thinly sliced carrot coin

1 slice cheese

1 slice steamed purple potato

1   Use the paring knife to make zigzag cuts around the middle of the yellow wax cover of the Babybel cheese. Gently pull the top half apart.

2   Using small micro tip scissors or a nori punch, cut two small dots out of nori to make the eyes.

3   Use an oval cutter to make the beak out of carrot. Make a tiny incision in the middle of the beak with the help of a paring knife.

4   Cut the feet out of carrot with a cutter.

5   Use a flower cutter and a round cutter to make a small pretty flower out of purple potato and cheese.

6   Place the little Babybel chick in a mini muffin cup. Decorate the head with the purple potato flower.

CHEEKY PIGLET BENTO

Who doesn't love adorable, little piglets? These happy ham piggies are sitting on top of pretty cheese daisies and yukari-flavoured onigiri. Yukari is a type of rice sprinkles made from red perilla leaves, salt and sugar. When you mix rice with yukari, the rice would turn purple and smell beautifully aromatic!

HAM PIGLETS ON DAISIES
MAKES 1

¼ slice ham
1 slice cheese
1 small piece nori seaweed
ketchup

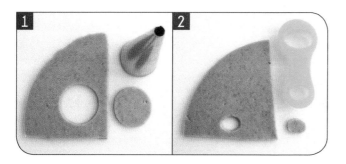

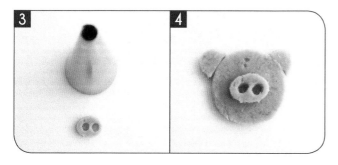

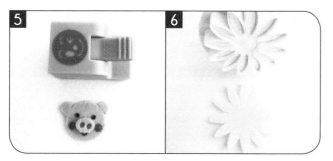

CONTENTS

Ham Piglets on Cheese Daisies
Yukari-Flavoured Onigiri
Crab and Cabbage Salad – 86
Simmered Black Beans – 94
Soy Sauce Eggs – 95
Cherry Tomatoes
Carrot Flowers

EQUIPMENT

assortment of cutters
nori punch
small knife
toothpick

1. Use a round decorating tip (bottom part) or a round cookie cutter to cut the piglet's head out of a slice of ham.

2. Use an oval cutter to cut the snout.

3. Punch two snout holes using a round decorating tip or a thin drinking straw.

4. Make another ham oval with the oval cutter and then cut it in half to make the ears. Attach the ears and snout to the piglet's head.

5. Use a smiley punch to cut the eyes and smile out of nori. Dab on rosy ketchup cheeks with a toothpick.

6. Cut a daisy flower out of cheese with a daisy / sunflower cutter. Place the ham piglet on top of the cheese daisy and you're done!

TIP

You can make yukari-flavoured onigiri by mixing yukari (see page 101) with steamed white or brown rice. Shape the rice into a ball or any other shape you like.

ELMO BENTO

Elmo is a furry red monster from the popular children's TV show "Sesame Street". These three Elmos are made out of crab sticks commonly used as the filling for California sushi rolls. If you cannot find crab sticks anywhere, substitute with cherry tomatoes or other ingredients with similar shape and colour.

CRAB STICK ELMOS

MAKES 3

1 crab stick
1 small piece nori seaweed
1 thinly sliced carrot coin
1 slice cheese
1 uncooked spaghetti noodle

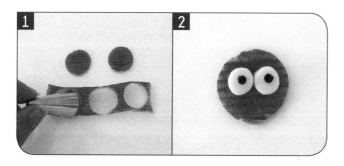

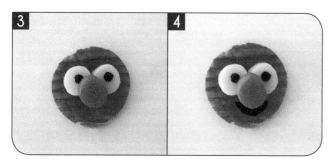

TIP

To make edible Elmos out of cherry tomatoes, follow Steps 2 – 4 and substitute Step 1 with cherry tomatoes.

CONTENTS

Crab Stick Elmos
Plain Onigiri
Spicy String Beans – 91
Prawn Cakes – 93
Steamed Corn
Steamed Broccoli
Cherry Tomato

EQUIPMENT

round cutter
thin drinking straw
nori punch
small scissors, or sharp knife

1   Cut three circles out of crab stick with the round cutter (if you do not have a small round cutter, use the bottom part of a decorating tip, or a fat straw).

2   Use the thin drinking straw to cut two small circles out of cheese for the eyes. Punch out two nori eyes and place them on top of the cheese eyes, or substitute the nori eyes with roasted black sesame seeds for a quicker alternative.

3   Cut out a round carrot nose with the thin drinking straw and attach by sticking a small piece of spaghetti through the carrot nose and into the rice ball.

4   Make the smile by cutting a semicircle shape out of nori.

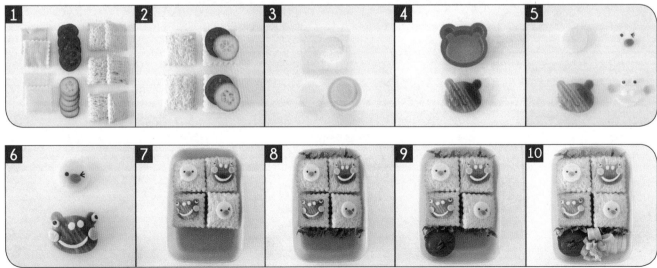

MINI FROG + CHICK SANDWICH BENTO

These mini sandwiches are very fun to make and they are also ideal for tea parties. Kids and grown-ups alike would adore them! Fill them with your favourite fillings and try other shapes, such as circles or triangles when cutting out the sandwiches.

CONTENTS

Mini Frog & Chick Sandwiches

Ham Flower

Carrot Flowers

Tulip Hard-Boiled Egg

Cucumber Slices

Cherry Tomato

Fruit

EQUIPMENT

assortment of cutters

nori punch

small scissors

MINI FROG + CHICK SANDWICHES

MAKES 4

TURKEY + CHEESE SANDWICHES

2 slices bread

4 slices smoked turkey or ham

2 slices cheese

2 cherry tomatoes, sliced

¼ small cucumber, sliced

1 tsp butter, softened

FROG + CHICK TOPPERS

2 cucumber peels (6x6 cm) – note: the size of the cucumber peels depends on how big or small your frog cutter is.

1 slice cheese (Cheddar or Gouda)

1 thinly sliced carrot coin

1 slice smoked ham

1 small piece nori seaweed

1. Slice the cherry tomatoes and cucumber thinly and cut stamp shapes out of the bread, cheese and smoked turkey.

2. Spread on butter or other condiments you like and add cucumber slices, tomatoes and a layer of cheese and turkey to the bread. Top with another slice of bread cutout.

3. Using a small circle cutter, cut out the cheese to make the chick's head.

4. To make the frog, use a teddy bear cutter to cut out the cucumber peel.

5. Use a nori punch to cut the chick's and frog's eyes out of nori seaweed and a round decorating tip to cut out the frog's (white) eyes, nostrils and smile. Punch the frog's rosy cheeks out of ham using a thin drinking straw, and cut the chick's beak out of carrot with small scissors or a mini oval cutter.

6. Attach the face details onto the chick and frog cutouts with a tiny dab of mayonnaise.

7. Top each mini sandwich with a cucumber frog or a cheese chick and secure with little pieces of uncooked spaghetti. Place them carefully into a bento box.

8. Add some lettuce border around the sandwiches.

9. Add a cherry tomato.

10. Fill the empty space of the box with a few slices of cucumber and a piece of ham flower.

TIP

Carefully wrap the mini sandwiches individually with plastic wrap to make sure that the frog and chick cutouts stay intact and won't move around during transportation.

PINK CHICK BENTO

Make adorable pink and white mini chicks out of quail eggs and place them in the bento box of your loved ones for a nice, little surprise. To make sure that the quail egg chicks stay intact during transport, use little pieces of uncooked spaghetti noodle to attach the quail eggs to the rice. After a few hours, the noodles will be soft and edible, due to moisture from the rice.

CONTENTS

Quail Egg Chicks

Tulip Hard-Boiled Egg

Deli Meat Flower

Cheese Flowers

Lettuce & Parsley

EQUIPMENT

nori punch

small paring knife

tweezers

TIP

To make beetroot juice, peel and dice one medium size beetroot. Place in a small saucepan, then cover with 100 ml water. Turn heat on high until water begins to boil. Turn heat to low and cook beetroot for another 2 minutes. Remove the beetroot pieces and retain the water to dye the quail eggs.

This method to create natural food dye can also be applied to other vegetables, such as purple carrots and red cabbage.

QUAIL EGG CHICKS
MAKES 4

4 quail eggs, boiled and peeled

beetroot juice

1 small piece nori seaweed

1 slice cheddar cheese

1   Soak 2 of the quail eggs in beetroot juice for 10 minutes (soak longer, if you want a darker colour).

2   Punch the eyes out of nori and gently arrange onto the white and pink quail eggs.

3   Use paring knife to cut little beaks out of the cheddar cheese and use a dab of mayonnaise to hold the beaks in place.

4   Your mini quail egg chicks are ready to serve!

THREE LITTLE PIGS BENTO

I love making piggies so much, I have to feature another piggy-themed bento: piggy onigiri filled with delicious chicken teriyaki. Other common onigiri fillings include tuna with mayonnaise, pickled plums, salted salmon, fried chicken and so on. The possibilities are endless!

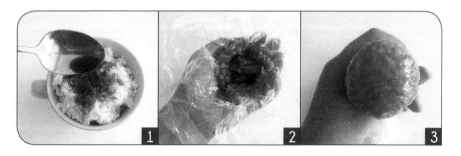

1   To make pink rice: mix steamed rice with beetroot juice to create pink-hued rice for the piggies' heads.

2   Divide the pink rice into 3 portions (around 3 tablespoons per rice ball). Place one portion of pink rice in the centre of a plastic wrap. Tuck 1 to 2 pieces chicken teriyaki into the centre of the rice and gather the plastic wrap up so that the rice surrounds the filling

3   Twist and squeeze the plastic wrap, forming a ball.

4   Make the snout out of smoked turkey using a round decorating tip.

5   Cut a circle out of turkey and slice it in half to make the ears.

6   Using small scissors, cut two round nori eyes.

7   Punch two rosy cheeks out of carrot with the round decorating tip or a thin drinking straw.

TIP

Try other red or orange coloured food items such as ham, salami, radish, crab sticks and tomato ketchup to make the rosy cheeks!

CONTENTS

EQUIPMENT

round decorating tip

small scissors

kitchen knife

1 sheet plastic wrap

PIGGY ONIGIRI

MAKES 3

PINK RICE

9 Tbsp steamed rice

2 Tbsp beetroot juice

CHICKEN TERIYAKI

50 g chicken thighs, deboned

1 Tbsp soy sauce

1 Tbsp sake

1 Tbsp mirin

¼ tsp sugar

Cut chicken into bite size pieces. Heat up a skillet and add a little oil. Pan-fry the chicken pieces until nicely browned and cooked through. Add soy sauce, sake, mirin and sugar and bring the sauce to a boil, while flipping the chicken repeatedly to coat evenly. Turn off the heat when the sauce has formed a thick glaze

FACIAL DETAILS

1 small piece nori seaweed

1 slice smoked turkey

1 thinly sliced carrot coin

BROWN BEAR BURGER PICNIC BENTO

These ridiculously cute burgers are filled with flavoursome teriyaki-style beef patties, fresh sliced tomatoes, crunchy lettuce and Japanese mayonnaise. I can imagine that these burgers would be a huge hit at children's parties! Change the fillings as you like, that's what makes a homemade burger fun!

CONTENTS

Brown Bear Burgers

Steamed Mixed Vegetables

Steamed Broccoli Florets

Babybel Cheese

Ham Flower

Fruit

EQUIPMENT

round cutters

nori punch

small scissors

tweezers

1   Fill the muffins (or hamburger buns) with the beef patties, lettuce, tomatoes and mayonnaise.

2   Place two round cheese cutouts on top of each muffin.

3   Cut two circles out of nori with small scissors and place them on top of the round cheese cutouts.

4   Make another round cheese cutout for the nose and two smaller ones for the eyes.

5   Place a small nori circle on top of the cheese nose.

6   Punch out the nori mouth with a nori punch or cut it out manually with scissors.

7   Make rosy cheeks by punching two circles out of smoked ham or blanched carrot with a small round cutter or a thin drinking straw.

8   Cut a circle out of cheese using a fat drinking straw or the bigger round cookie cutter used previously in steps 2 and 4. Slice the circle in half to make the ears and attach on the top right and left corners of the muffin.

BROWN BEAR BURGERS
MAKES 3

3 English muffins, halved

lettuce

sliced tomatoes

mayonnaise

1 slice cheese

1 small piece nori seaweed

¼ slice smoked ham

BEEF PATTIES

350 g ground beef

½ onion, minced

1 egg, beaten

4 Tbsp breadcrumbs

2 Tbsp oyster sauce

½ tsp garlic powder

1 Tbsp dried oregano

pinch black pepper

SWEET SAUCE

3 Tbsp soy sauce

½ – 1 Tbsp sugar

3 Tbsp white wine

4 Tbsp water

Place all ingredients for the beef patties in a large bowl. Mix with your hands until evenly combined. Divide into 3 portions. Shape each portion into a thin patty. Pan-fry both side of the patties until golden brown and cooked through.

Add soy sauce, white wine, water and sugar. Let the mixture boil, while flipping the patties repeatedly to coat evenly. When the sauce has formed a thick glaze around the patties, turn off the heat and set the patties aside.

TIP

Make sure to fold the nori seaweed piece in half before cutting out the nori eyes with scissors. This will ensure that you will get two equal nori circles. If you don't like the taste of nori, use black olives for the eyes instead!

CHEERFUL MONKEY BENTO

This lovely monkey onigiri is proof that no special bento tools and equipments are necessary to make a creative and presentable edible creation. If you don't have a cookie cutter, use a toothpick to cut out cheese in any way you like. There are so many everyday kitchen equipments you can use to substitute those fancy and sometimes pricey bento gears! Think outside the box and you will get there!

CONTENTS

Monkey Onigiri

EQUIPMENT

fat drinking straw

thin drinking straw

small scissors

1 sheet plastic wrap

toothpick

MONKEY ONIGIRI

MAKES 1

5 Tbsp steamed rice

2 boiled egg yolks

1 slice cheese

1 small piece nori seaweed

1 thinly sliced carrot coin

> ### TIP
>
> Alternatively, instead of using egg yolks to colour the rice yellow, you can also try turmeric or curry powder to give the rice a yellow shade. Check out page 84 for a delicious Indonesian-style turmeric rice recipe.

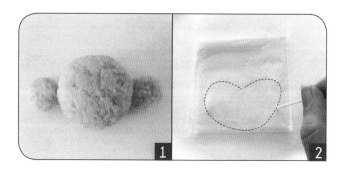

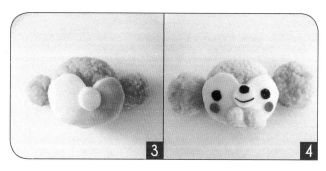

1   To make yellow rice: mix steamed rice with the boiled egg yolks until well combined. Take 3 tablespoons of the yellow rice and shape into a ball with a sheet of plastic wrap to make the head. Make the ears using 1½ tablespoons yellow rice.

2   Use a toothpick to cut cheese into a heart shape for the monkey's face.

3   Make a small round cheese cutout for the nose with a fat drinking straw.

4   Using small scissors, cut the eyes, nose and smile out of nori seaweed and cut out the rosy carrot cheeks with a thin drinking straw. Lastly, use the remaining ½ tablespoon yellow rice to make the hands.

FRIENDLY POLAR BEAR BENTO

If you own a teddy bear cutter and a nori punch, these egg white polar bears will be a piece of cake to make. Egg whites are also high in quality protein, contain little calories and are free of fats and cholesterol. They will make great toppings for any savoury bentos and will surely make anyone who receives the bento squeals with delight!

EQUIPMENT

bear cutter

nori punch

round decorating tip

toothpick

tweezers

BOILED EGG WHITE POLAR BEARS

MAKES 4

4 slices boiled egg white

1 small piece nori seaweed

tomato ketchup

CONTENTS

Boiled Egg White Polar Bears

Mini Chick Onigiri

Seafood & Vermicelli Salad – 87

Coconut Chicken – 92

Indonesian-Style Fried Rice – 85

Nori Seaweed, to cover the fried rice

Steamed Mixed Vegetables

Steamed Broccoli Florets

1 Cut a teddy bear shape out of a slice of boiled egg white with the bear cutter.

2 Punch out a round egg white nose with the decorating tip and place it in the middle of the bear's face.

3 Cut out the nori facial details with a nori punch and apply these carefully with tweezers.

4 Dab on rosy ketchup cheeks with a toothpick. Make more polar bears with the rest of the egg white slices.

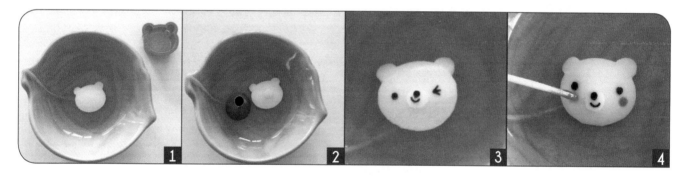

TIP

Place a portion of fried rice into the left side of the bento box and cover the rice with a piece of nori seaweed before topping it with the egg white polar bears (see 5).

The two mini chick onigiri are made the same way as the monkey onigiri on page 39. Shape the egg yolk flavoured rice into 2 tiny balls, add the nori facial details and carrot beaks. Lastly, decorate the chicks with hat food picks (see 6).

FLUFFY BEAR ONIGIRI BENTO

I made these fluffy bear onigiri for my little niece, who adores fish floss. I don't think you would be able to get fish floss easily from your local Asian grocery store, but you may be able to find some beef floss products which have the same fuzzy texture as the fish floss I used for this bento. You can also substitute the fish floss with *katsuoboshi* or bonito flakes, which are often used in Japanese cooking to make dashi broth or as topping for savoury Japanese snacks, such as takoyaki and okonomiyaki. If beef floss or *katsuoboshi* is not your cup of tea, simply season the rice with a few drops of soy sauce to achieve similar brown colour. However your bear rice balls will not have the same fluffy texture as pictured. You can also be adventurous and try other colours and textures. After all, a bear doesn't always have to be brown, especially not in the bento world!

CONTENTS

Fluffy Bear Onigiri	
Spicy Rice Cakes – 94	
Vegetable & Beef Rolls – 94	
Basic Tamagoyaki – 97	
Blanched Broccoli Florets	

FLUFFY BEAR ONIGIRI
MAKES 1

3 Tbsp steamed rice
fish floss
1 slice cheese
1 small piece nori seaweed
1 thinly sliced carrot coin
1 uncooked spaghetti noodle

EQUIPMENT

round cutter
nori punch
1 sheet plastic wrap

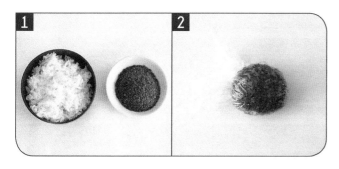

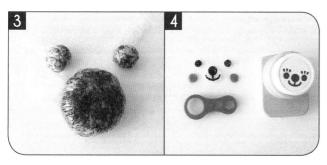

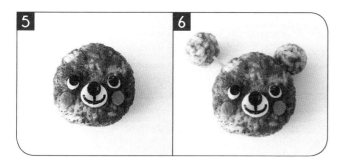

1. Mix steamed rice and fish floss with a spoon.

2. Put 2 ½ tablespoons fish floss-flavoured rice in the centre of a plastic wrap and gather the plastic wrap around the rice. Firmly press the rice into a round shape.

3. Make two mini balls out of the remaining fish floss rice using the same technique as step 2.

4. Cut the facial details out of cheese, nori and carrot.

5. Place the eyes, nose and rosy cheeks onto the bear.

6. Attach each ear with a small piece of uncooked spaghetti noodle.

BASHFUL BUNNY BENTO

If you have been following my blog, I am sure you know that I love rabbits. I think they are the sweetest animals on earth! If you have a pet rabbit, I believe you know what I am talking about. They are intelligent creatures with some quirky personalities! If you know anyone who are crazy about rabbits, make this bento for them to make their day!

BUNNY ONIGIRI
MAKES 1

3 Tbsp steamed rice
1 slice smoked turkey, or cheese
1 slice smoked ham
1 piece nori seaweed
1 thinly sliced carrot coin

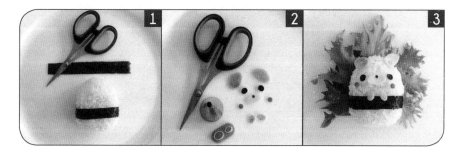

1   Place the rice into a sheet of plastic wrap. Gather up the ends of the plastic wrap. Twist and squeeze tightly to form an oval. Cut a thin strip of nori seaweed and wrap the tummy of the bunny onigiri with the nori strip.

2   Cut out the smoked turkey eyes using a round decorating tip and top with two round nori eyes. Use the bigger oval cutter to cut out the ham ears and smoked turkey nose. Punch out the ham paws with the smaller oval cutter and make the rosy cheeks by cutting two tiny circles out of blanched carrot with the decorating tip. Lastly, top the smoked turkey nose with a black nori dot.

3   Place the facial features on top of the bunny onigiri as pictured.

CONTENTS

EQUIPMENT

round decorating tip
mini oval cutters
small scissors
1 sheet plastic wrap

TIP

If you don't have any oval cutters, use drinking straws to create oval shapes by slightly pinching the straws when cutting out cheese, deli meat or cooked vegetables.

FUNKY PENGUIN BENTO

No worries! No penguins have been harmed in the making of this penguin-themed bento box, these are only precious penguin-shaped rice balls wrapped in nori seaweed and decorated with cute hat food picks! Savour these darling penguin onigiri together with delicious wontons, simmered potatoes and tasty sweet pepper chicken or other bento fillers of your choice.

CONTENTS

Penguin onigiri

Steamed Broccoli Florets

EQUIPMENT

small scissors

round decorating tips

small oval cutter

1 sheet plastic wrap

1 Put 3 tablespoons rice in the centre of a plastic wrap and gather the plastic wrap around the rice. Firmly press the rice into an oval shape.

2 Remove the rice from the plastic wrap and place it on a piece of nori seaweed.

3 Gather the nori seaweed around the rice.

4 Wrap the nori covered rice with the previously used plastic wrap. Twist the plastic wrap to make sure that the nori seaweed fully seals the rice ball.

5 Prepare the facial details using nori, cheese and blanched carrot. If you don't have an oval cutter, use a fat drinking straw to cut out the carrot beak and feet by slightly pinching the straw to create an oval shape.

6 Use small pieces of spaghetti noodle to attach the cheese and carrot cutouts to the rice and stick the nori eyes with a dab of mayonnaise

PENGUIN ONIGIRI

MAKES 1

3 Tbsp steamed rice

1 slice cheese

½ piece nori seaweed (18 x 10 cm), to wrap the rice

1 small piece nori seaweed, for the eyes

1 thinly sliced carrot coin

1 uncooked spaghetti noodle

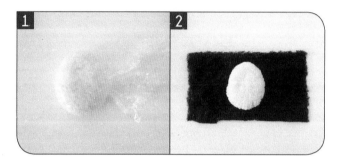

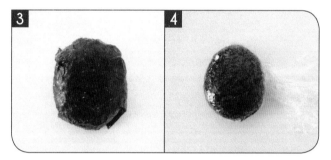

LOVELY LION BENTO

As a kid I would be ecstatic to find an edible friendly-looking lion in my lunchbox. After all lions are such gorgeous animals! The brown onigiri which makes the lion's head is just rice seasoned with soy sauce. If you think that it's too plain, fill the onigiri with anything you like. To see how to fill an onigiri, check out page 100.

CONTENTS

Lion Onigiri

Steamed Chicken & Vegetable Meatballs – 93

Steamed Broccoli Florets

Boiled Edamame Beans

Almonds

Fruit

EQUIPMENT

round cutters

small scissors

nori punch

1 sheet plastic wrap

LION ONIGIRI

MAKES 1

SOY SAUCE RICE

3 Tbsp steamed rice

1 tsp soy sauce

SPAGHETTI MANE

your favourite spaghetti recipe

FACIAL DETAILS

1 small piece nori seaweed

1 slice smoked turkey

1 thinly sliced carrot coin

4 small pieces fried spaghetti

TIP

To make the fried spaghetti whiskers, simply fry small pieces of spaghetti in oil until golden brown.

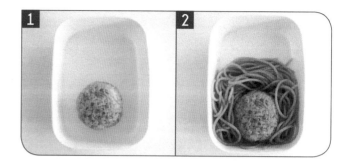

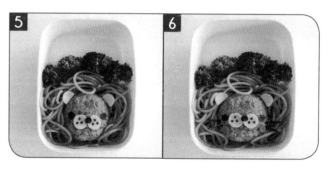

1   Mix 3 tablespoons steamed rice with 1 teaspoon soy sauce until well combined. Shape the rice into a ball with a plastic wrap, remove the wrap and place the onigiri into a bento box.

2   Arrange the spaghetti noodles to make the mane.

3   Add the nori eyes, which you can make with a nori punch or little micro-tip scissors.

4   Make the snout by adding 2 round smoked turkey circles, 6 tiny nori circle cutouts and 1 bigger round nori cutout for the middle nose.

5   Punch a circle out of smoked turkey and cut it in half to make the ears.

6   Add the rosy carrot cheeks and the fried spaghetti whiskers.

TRADITIONAL BENTO

52
LOW-CARB
PORK CUTLET BENTO

54
SESAME
STEAK BENTO

56
BRAISED
DUCK BENTO

58
CHICKEN CUTLET
BENTO

60
GINGER PORK
BENTO

62
EBI FRY
BENTO

64
CHICKEN SOBORO
BENTO

66
SHRIMP + CUCUMBER RICE
BENTO

68
GARLIC CHICKEN + MAKI SUSHI
BENTO

70
MUSHROOM + PORK
UDON BENTO

72
SZECHUAN-STYLE
SPAGHETTI BENTO

74
SPAGHETTI BOLOGNESE
BENTO

76
DUCK
FRIED RICE BENTO

78
JAPANESE-INSPIRED
CHICKEN + AVOCADO SALAD BENTO

80
BEEF RENDANG
BENTO

LOW-CARB PORK CUTLET BENTO

These mini pork cutlets are a good alternative for people who love schnitzel or the Japanese variant, *tonkatsu*, but want to consume less carbohydrate, as the cutlets are coated with almond flour instead of the usual flour, egg and breadcrumbs mixture. If you want to make this bento lunch set a real low-carb bento, you can omit the rice and turtle-shaped pasta and change it with salad greens instead.

CONTENTS

BEEF BULGOGI WITH SHIMEJI MUSHROOMS

4 SERVINGS

500 g thinly sliced beef

200 g shimeji mushrooms

4 Tbsp soy sauce

3 Tbsp dry sherry

1 Tbsp sugar

½ pear, minced

½ Tbsp honey

1 Tbsp sesame oil

1 Tbsp roasted sesame seeds

2 stalks green onions, chopped

3 cloves garlic, minced

1 onion, sliced

2 Tbsp cooking oil

Mix all ingredients together (except the Shimeji mushrooms and roasted sesame seeds) and marinate for 2 hours.

Sauté the beef in the oil. Add the Shimeji mushrooms and cook for 2 – 3 minutes. Serve and garnish with roasted sesame seeds.

LOW-CARB PORK CUTLETS

1– 2 SERVINGS

150 g pork fillet

2 Tbsp soy sauce

1 Tbsp minced garlic

1 egg

½ tsp stevia (optional)

100 g almond flour

oil for pan-frying

Cut the pork fillet into thin slices. Combine the remaining ingredients except the almond flour, and rub onto the pork slices. Marinate for 15 – 30 minutes. Dredge the pork in the almond flour. Pan-fry until both sides are cooked and golden brown.

LOW-CARB PORK CUTLETS

SESAME STEAK BENTO

Imagine having steak in your lunchbox. I know I would be very happy! Instead of the usual French fries or other potato-based side dishes, why don't you give steamed rice a go? Steak seasoned with sesame oil goes very well with rice. Top the rice with soft pickled plum, or *umeboshi* in Japanese, and pickled ginger for a nice extra kick!

CONTENTS

SESAME STEAK

1 SERVING

100 g beef steak

2 Tbsp sesame oil

1 Tbsp minced garlic

1 Tbsp soy sauce

1 Tbsp red wine

freshly ground pepper, to taste

Heat sesame oil over medium heat. Sauté the garlic until fragrant and add the steak. Cook until both sides are lightly brown. Stir in the red wine and cook until the steak is well done.

Sprinkle with soy sauce and freshy ground pepper. Cut into strips.

SESAME MIXED GREEN SALAD

1 SERVING

30 g mixed salad greens

4 cherry tomatoes, halved

1 Tbsp chopped red onion

1 Tbsp sesame oil

1 tsp soy sauce

freshly ground pepper, to taste

Toss sesame oil and soy sauce with the mixed salad greens, chopped red onion and cherry tomatoes. Sprinkle with freshly ground pepper.

PICKLED PLUM ASPARAGUS

1 – 2 SERVINGS

2 stalks asparagus, blanched

1 umeboshi, minced

½ Tbsp soy sauce

1 Tbsp sesame oil

freshly ground pepper, to taste

Cut the blanched asparagus into 3 cm lengths. Season with minced umeboshi, soy sauce, sesame oil and pepper. Mix well.

PICKLED PLUM ASPARAGUS

BRAISED DUCK BENTO

I made this bento in 2012. I have blogged briefly about it, but I still want to feature this bento in this cookbook, because it belongs to one of my most favourite bento creations. It is pretty basic, but I love the food arrangement – this bento shows how a simple vegetable cutter could transform a rather plain bento meal into something rather extravagant. The cute tomberries certainly do play a role in making this bento prettier as well. However, I realise that tomberries are not widely available everywhere, but you still can achieve a similar result by using other vegetables with similar colours, such as cherry tomatoes and yellow sweet peppers. Slice them thinly and arrange them neatly on top of the rice.

CONTENTS

Braised Duck

Pan-Fried Teriyaki Scotch Egg

Tomberries (Miniature Tomatoes)

Carrot Butterflies

Steamed Brown Rice – 84

Roasted Black Sesame Seeds

Cucumber "Leaves"

Blackberry

Radish

BRAISED DUCK

2 SERVINGS

2 duck breasts (about 150 g each)

250 ml water

1 Tbsp fish sauce

10 Tbsp soy sauce

½ tsp cinnamon powder

2 star anise pods

2 Tbsp sugar, or to taste

3 garlic cloves, crushed

pinch ground pepper

Pan-fry the duck breasts until both sides are golden brown. Meanwhile, mix together the rest of the ingredients in a pot, and bring to a boil.

Place the duck breasts into the marinade and reduce the heat to medium-low. Simmer for 40 minutes until the meat is tender. Slice into serving pieces.

PAN-FRIED TERIYAKI SCOTCH EGGS

4 SERVINGS

2 hard-boiled eggs, cooled & peeled

200 g ground meat

1 egg, beaten

½ Tbsp chicken stock powder

1 tsp fish sauce

pinch ground pepper

2 Tbsp breadcrumbs

2 Tbsp flour

extra flour for dusting

4 Tbsp soy sauce

1 Tbsp sugar

oil for pan-frying

Combine ground meat, chicken stock powder, fish sauce, beaten egg, pepper, breadcrumbs and flour together. Mix well and divide into 2 equal portions.

Pat one portion of the ground meat mixture into a thin patty. Lay one hard-boiled egg on top of the patty and wrap the patty around the egg with your floured hand. Repeat with the other hard-boiled egg. Pan-fry the scotch eggs until all sides are golden brown. Add soy sauce and sugar. Mix well and make sure that the scotch eggs are well coated with the sauce. When the sauce has started to get sticky, turn off the heat. Cut the scotch eggs in half and serve.

PAN-FRIED SCOTCH EGGS

CHICKEN CUTLET BENTO

Most people I know love good, crunchy deep-fried food. Definitely not very healthy, but from time to time, I like to treat myself to some delicious deep-fried goodies, and Japanese-style chicken cutlets are one of them. Serve on top of rice and eat together with a portion of refreshing salad and Japanese pickles.

CONTENTS

SAUTÉED PAK CHOI

1 SERVING

1 baby pak choi, quartered

1 Tbsp Shaoxing wine, or sherry

½ Tbsp soy sauce

½ Tbsp oyster sauce

sesame oil

Heat 1 tablespoon sesame oil in a frying pan. When hot, add pak choi and stir-fry for a few seconds. Quickly add Shaoxing wine and coat with soy sauce and oyster sauce. Finish with a drizzle of sesame oil.

LETTUCE + TOMATO SALAD

2 SERVINGS

50 g lettuce

1 tomato, thinly sliced

2 Tbsp olive oil

3 Tbsp lemon juice

1 tsp apple cider vinegar

¼ tsp dried basil

1 tsp sugar, or to taste

freshly ground black pepper, to taste

Toss lettuce and the tomato slices together and season with olive oil, lemon juice, vinegar, dried basil, sugar and pepper.

PORK + CHIVES DUMPLINGS

MAKES 30

200 g ground pork

5 Tbsp chopped garlic chives

1 tsp grated ginger

2 Tbsp oyster sauce

1 Tbsp fish sauce

½ tsp sugar

1 Tbsp Shaoxing wine, or sherry

1 Tbsp sesame oil

white pepper, to taste

30 round dumpling wrappers

Combine all of the ingredients except the dumpling wrappers in a bowl and mix well. Place 1 teaspoon of pork filling onto the centre of each wrapper. Fold the wrapper in half and seal it with water. Cook the dumplings in boiling water for 2 – 3 minutes.

CHICKEN CUTLETS

2 SERVINGS

2 skinless chicken thigh fillets (about 100 grams each)

1 Tbsp oyster sauce

1 Tbsp soy sauce

1 egg, beaten

pinch pepper

3 Tbsp flour

6 Tbsp panko bread crumbs

oil for frying

Pound each chicken fillet to equal thickness with a meat tenderizer. Set the egg, flour and bread crumbs in three different shallow bowls. Add oyster sauce, soy sauce and pepper to the egg bowl and mix well. Coat the chicken thigh fillets in the flour, then dip in the egg mixture and roll in the bread crumbs. Fry the chicken until golden brown. Transfer to a paper towel to drain.

> **TIP**
>
> Tonkatsu sauce and Japanese mayonnaise go really well with the chicken cutlets. Give this condiment combo a try!

GINGER PORK BENTO

Garlic and ginger make a wonderful and aromatic combination when stir-fried. This is a simple, homey dish which is perfect for people who love practical bento lunches. Add a few pieces of fresh cherry tomatoes, radishes, sweet pepper sticks and leafy greens for added flavour, colour and texture. You should also give the fried "pocket" eggs a try, if you want a different alternative to the usual sunny side ups or tamagoyaki.

CONTENTS

Ginger Pork Medallions

Fried "Pocket" Egg

Sautéed Mushrooms

Red Sweet Pepper Sticks

Cherry Tomatoes

Radishes

Salad Greens

Boiled Potato Flowers

Pickled Ginger

GINGER PORK MEDALLIONS

1 SERVING

100 g pork shoulder, sliced into 1 cm thickness

1 Tbsp olive oil

3 cloves garlic, thinly sliced

1 Tbsp grated ginger

1 ½ Tbsp soy sauce

½ tsp sugar

1 Tbsp chopped scallion

coarsely ground pepper, to taste

shichimi togarashi

Add olive oil to a well heated pan and sauté garlic and ginger until fragrant.

Add pork and sauté over medium high heat. Lightly season with soy sauce, sugar and pepper.

Garnish with chopped scallion and shichimi togarashi.

SAUTÉED MUSHROOMS

1 SERVING

6 button mushrooms, thinly sliced

1 tsp butter

¼ tsp minced garlic

1 Tbsp white wine

½ tsp soy sauce

1 tsp lemon juice

1 tsp chopped parsley

pepper, to taste

Sauté mushrooms in butter. Add garlic and cook and toss for around 20 seconds. Season with soy sauce, lemon juice, parsley and pepper.

FRIED "POCKET" EGGS

3 SERVINGS

3 eggs

oil for frying

½ Tbsp soy sauce, per egg

salt and pepper, to taste

Heat 1 Tbsp oil in a skillet over medium heat. Crack one egg into the skillet and fry until half-set. Add soy sauce and sprinkle some salt and pepper.

Fold the egg in half and fry until both sides are cooked and lightly brown. Repeat with the rest of the eggs. Cut each "pocket" egg into halves before serving.

EBI FRY BENTO

This is an easy, delicious bento dish, which is suitable and is a popular choice for everyday bento. Make big batches of *ebi fry*, another word for Japanese-style fried shrimps, in advance and freeze them. This will save you plenty of preparation time. Serve with steamed brown rice drizzled with mayonnaise and tonkatsu sauce, Korean-style bean sprouts, stir-fried water spinach, boiled egg, Japanese pickles (Shibazuke and Shisozuke) and fresh strawberries.

CONTENTS

Ebi Fry

Stir-Fried Water Spinach

Korean-Style Bean Sprouts

Spicy Egg

Carrot Bunny & Flowers

Shibazuke

Shisozuke

Fruit

EBI FRY

MAKES 12 EBI FRIES

12 large shrimps

150 g panko bread crumbs

5 Tbsp flour

1 egg, beaten

1 Tbsp oyster sauce

salt and pepper, to taste

Set the eggs, flour and bread crumbs in three different shallow bowls. Add oyster sauce, salt and pepper to the egg bowl and mix well.

One at a time, dredge the shrimp in the flour, then dip in the egg mixture and coat with the bread crumbs. Repeat the previous step one more time (optional).

Deep-fry the shrimps until golden brown.

KOREAN-STYLE BEAN SPROUTS

2 SERVINGS

100 g bean sprouts

1 Tbsp sesame oil

½ Tbsp soy sauce

¼ tsp sugar

½ Tbsp gochugaru

roasted sesame seeds

Clean and wash bean sprouts. Drain. Cook bean sprouts for 2 minutes.

Rinse bean sprouts with cold water and drain completely. Add sesame oil, soy sauce, hot pepper flakes, sugar and toasted sesame seeds. Mix well.

STIR-FRIED WATER SPINACH

1 – 2 SERVINGS

100 g water spinach, cut into 5 cm length

½ Tbsp sesame oil

½ Tbsp soy sauce

½ Tbsp fish sauce

½ Tbsp oyster sauce

black pepper, to taste

Heat sesame oil in a skillet over high heat. Add water spinach stems and stir-fry for 1 minute.

Add the leaves, soy sauce, fish sauce, oyster sauce and black pepper and toss for another one minute until the leaves wilt.

> **TIP**
>
> To make the spicy egg, cut one hard-boiled egg in half, sprinkle with shichimi togarashi (Japanese 7 spice powder) and sesame oil to taste.

CHICKEN SOBORO BENTO

Chicken Soboro or simmered ground chicken is commonly served in Japan as topping for rice. Often eaten together with scrambled egg and green vegetables, chicken soboro is one of my favourite bento fillings, as the recipe can be prepared quickly and easily. Feel free to use ground turkey, pork or beef instead of ground chicken, or even a vegetarian alternative, such as chopped tofu, tempeh, mushrooms or beans.

CONTENTS

Simmered Ground Chicken

Sautéed Snow Peas

Scrambled Egg

Cherry Tomatoes

Steamed White Rice – 84

Pickled Ginger

Radish

Fruit

CHICKEN SOBORO

1 SERVING

100g ground chicken

1 Tbsp soy sauce

1 Tbsp sake

1 Tbsp mirin

½ Tbsp oyster sauce

½ tsp sugar

½ Tbsp grated ginger

2 Tbsp sesame oil

4 Tbsp water

pinch white pepper

Place all of the ingredients in a pan. Mix well and cook over medium low heat, stirring occasionally to avoid clumping. Turn off the heat when the liquid is almost gone and the chicken is cooked through.

SCRAMBLED EGG

1 SERVING

1 egg, beaten

1 Tbsp mirin

½ tsp dashi powder

1 Tbsp oil

Mix the beaten egg with mirin and dashi powder. Add oil to a well heated pan. Pour the egg mixture and whisk vigorously with several chopsticks until crumbly.

SAUTÉED SNOW PEAS

1 SERVING

5 snow peas, sliced

½ tsp dashi powder

black pepper, to taste

1 Tbsp sesame oil

Add sesame oil to a well heated pan. Sauté the snow peas and season with dashi powder and pepper.

SHRIMP + CUCUMBER RICE BENTO

If you would like something light and refreshing for your lunch, you should definitely give this shrimp and cucumber rice a try. The cucumber slices add crunch and pleasantly fresh flavour to the vinegared rice. The pink lotus roots are also a terrific accompaniment to the rice – they are tangy, crunchy and very cooling. Since this is a rather mild rice dish, eat it together with plain blanched or steamed vegetables. Side dishes that are too well-seasoned will overpower the taste of the rice.

SHRIMP + CUCUMBER RICE

1 SERVING

150 g hot cooked rice

8 - 10 boiled shrimps

1 Tbsp chopped blanched carrot

¼ small cucumber, sliced into thin rounds

¼ tsp salt

1 Tbsp sesame oil

1 Tbsp vinegar

1 Tbsp soy sauce

pinch white pepper

roasted sesame seeds

¼ tsp aonori

Sprinkle the cucumber with salt, knead and squeeze out the liquid. Stir the cucumber slices into the rice together with the rest of the ingredients. Mix well.

PINK LOTUS ROOTS

3 SERVINGS

6 slices blanched lotus roots

2 leaves red cabbage, roughly chopped

juice from 1 lemon

2 Tbsp vinegar

2 Tbsp sugar

¼ tsp salt

150 ml water

Place the red cabbage leaves into a food processor and pour 150 ml water. Blend to form a smooth purée.

Pour the red cabbage purée into a sieve set up over a bowl. Boil the juice for 1 minute.

Add salt, sugar, vinegar and lemon juice to turn the liquid pink. Place the lotus root slices in the pink mixture and marinate in the fridge for 1 hour.

CONTENTS

TIP

Pink lotus roots are great for sandwiches and even hamburgers. They also taste wonderful when eaten together with spicy dishes.

GARLIC CHICKEN + MAKI SUSHI BENTO

I could have this bento everyday! It's chock-full of delicious goodies – pan-fried garlic chicken, maki sushi, tea eggs, carrot pickles and pretty leaf-shaped cucumber slices. I filled my maki sushi with garlic chicken, cucumber sticks and mayonnaise. But sushi rolls are so versatile, you can fill them with anything you want: smoked salmon, schnitzel, even ham and cheese! Just think of it like making your own sandwiches or bread rolls filled with your favourite ingredients!

CONTENTS

GARLIC CHICKEN

1 SERVING

150 g chicken fillet, cut into bite-size pieces

2 Tbsp soy sauce

1 Tbsp mirin

¼ tsp sugar

1 Tbsp minced garlic

pepper, to taste

1 egg

2 Tbsp flour

oil for pan-frying

Combine all ingredients and marinate for 15 minutes. Pan-fry the chicken pieces until both sides are golden brown. Lower the heat to medium and continue cooking for 1 more minute until the chicken pieces are cooked through.

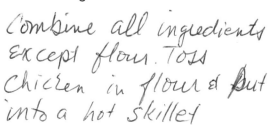
Combine all ingredients Except flour. Toss Chicken in flour & Put into a hot skillet

MAKI SUSHI

MAKES 1 SUSHI ROLL

200 g hot steamed rice

1½ Tbsp vinegar

¼ tsp salt

½ tsp sugar

1 nori sheet

mayonnaise, to taste

garlic chicken

cucumber sticks

Combine the rice with vinegar, salt and sugar. Mix well and then let cool.

Lay a sheet of nori on a sushi rolling mat. Spread out rice over the nori, leaving about 2 cm strip of nori at the bottom.

Place the garlic chicken, cucumber sticks and mayonnaise on the rice and roll until you reach the end of the rice. Glue the remaining seaweed with a few grains of rice and finish rolling.

Use a sharp knife and cut the sushi roll into 6 – 8 pieces.

MUSHROOM + PORK UDON BENTO

How I love noodles! I have been eating noodles for as long as I can remember. I love noodles so much that one of my aunts used to jokingly tell me that my hair would get as curly as ramen due to noodles overconsumption – which I wouldn't mind really, since I quite fancy curly hair. But, since most noodles aren't curly anyway, my hair has always remained straight. One of my most favourite noodle types is udon. I just love its soft, chewy texture and versatility. Udon tastes great both in soups and stir-fried. The recipe below shows my version of stir-fried udon, which is normally called *Yaki udon* in Japanese.

CONTENTS

Mushroom & Pork Udon

Blanched Asparagus

Pickled Ginger

MUSHROOM + PORK UDON

1 SERVING

200 g udon noodles

80 g ground pork

5 button mushrooms, thinly sliced

2 Tbsp sesame oil

1 Tbsp sake

1 Tbsp soy sauce

1 Tbsp oyster sauce

½ tsp sugar

1 Tbsp chopped scallion

white pepper, to taste

pickled ginger

Add sesame oil to a heated pan. Add ground pork and mushrooms. Stir-fry until lightly browned.

Season with sake, soy sauce, oyster sauce and sugar. Stir-fry for another minute. Add udon noodles. Coat noodles well with the sauce. Turn heat to high and stir briefly.

Add chopped scallion and white pepper to taste. Garnish with Japanese red pickled ginger.

SZECHUAN-STYLE SPAGHETTI BENTO

I have mentioned my love for noodles in the previous page. Spaghetti is no exception. Besides making traditional Italian pasta dishes, I love to experiment and create fusion pasta, combining the flavours of East and West. This Szechuan-style spaghetti is one good example. Szechuan is a province in Southwestern China well known for its hot and spicy specialties. If you love to try something new and adore spicy food, this is definitely a must-try!

CONTENTS

Szechuan-Style Spaghetti

Blanched Pak Choi

Steamed Purple Potato Flower

Carrot Flowers

Radish

SZECHUAN-STYLE SPAGHETTI

1 SERVING

100 g spaghetti

6 button mushrooms, thinly sliced

50 g ground pork

1 Tbsp olive oil

2 red chili peppers, de-seeded & chopped

1 Tbsp minced garlic

1 Tbsp oyster sauce

2 Tbsp hot chili oil

1 Tbsp peanut butter

½ tsp sugar

1 Tbsp chopped green onions

white pepper, to taste

Boil spaghetti according to package directions until al dente. Set aside.

Coat a well heated pan with olive oil. Add minced garlic and chili pepper and stir-fry until fragrant.

Add ground pork and mushroom slices. Stir-fry until pork is lightly brown. Season with oyster sauce, peanut butter, hot chili oil and sugar. Add spaghetti and coat the noodles well with the meat sauce. Finish with chopped green onions and white pepper to taste.

Serve with blanched pak choi or any other leafy vegetables of your choice, a piece of radish and carrot flowers

SPAGHETTI BOLOGNESE BENTO

Spaghetti Bolognese is one of my favourite pasta dishes. Everyone has their own special recipe for making the Bolognese sauce and this is how I like to prepare mine. If you don't like beef or are not allowed to eat beef due to any reasons, try ground pork or chicken. I have tried both alternatives and they both make equally good Bolognese sauce.

CONTENTS

Spaghetti Bolognese

Blanched Asparagus

Cheese Flowers

Ham Flowers

Sweet Pepper

Fruit

SPAGHETTI BOLOGNESE

2 – 3 SERVINGS

300 g spaghetti

300 g ground beef

2 Tbsp olive oil

1 Tbsp minced garlic

1 onion, finely chopped

1 carrot, finely chopped

1 can (240 g) peeled tomatoes

1 Tbsp tomato paste

200 g cream

250 ml red wine

1 Tbsp chopped basil

1 Tbsp chopped oregano

chicken stock powder, to taste

pepper and sugar, to taste

grated parmesan cheese

Add olive oil to a heated pan and sauté the minced garlic over low heat. When the garlic is lightly browned, add chopped onion, carrot and ground meat.

When the meat is just cooked, stir in the red wine. Add the canned tomatoes, tomato paste and cream. Simmer the sauce over medium heat.

Season with chopped basil and oregano, and add chicken powder, sugar and pepper to taste.

Meanwhile, cook spaghetti in a large saucepan of boiling water, following package directions until al dente. Serve pasta with the sauce, topped with parmesan cheese.

TIP

Decorate the pasta with blanched asparagus and ham flowers, and sprinkle with dried oregano

Use a baran (food divider) or a food cup to separate the fruit from the pasta.

Use two different size sunflower cutters to make the yellow flowers out of cheese. The round part can be easily made with a circle cutter.

DUCK FRIED RICE BENTO

This bento looks quite time consuming to prepare, but in fact this is one of those bentos which can be assembled pretty easily. The recipe for this duck fried rice doesn't require too many ingredients, that's why it is perfect for a quick bento fix. If you are using freshly cooked rice, make sure to let it cool first or chill in the refrigerator for a a few hours beforehand. Stir-frying soft, sticky rice is very tricky and you might end up with mushy, unappetising fried rice.

I also used store-bought chicken cordon bleu, as I was short on time when I was making this bento. There are plenty of suitable bento fillers at your local supermarket's frozen food aisle, think chicken popcorns, potato wedges or fish fingers. Nevertheless I have included my favourite chicken cordon bleu recipe below for you to recreate at home. Even though store-bought food is convenient, homemade food is still the best!

CONTENTS

Easy Duck Fried Rice

Chicken Cordon Bleu

Basic Tamagoyaki – 97

Ham Roses

Cucumber Slices

Boiled Edamame Beans

Baby Carrots

Cherry Tomatoes

Cheese Flowers

Radish

Fruit

EASY DUCK FRIED RICE

1 SERVINGS

200 g cooked rice, chilled

2 Tbsp olive oil

100 g duck breast, cut into bite-size pieces

1 ½ Tbsp fish sauce

2 Tbsp oyster sauce

1 Tbsp sweet soy sauce

½ tsp white pepper

1 egg

3 Tbsp chopped green onions

Heat up your wok to high and add olive oil. Add duck and fish sauce and stir-fry for 1 minute. Quickly toss in rice, oyster sauce and sweet soy sauce. Stir fry for another 1 minute. Push rice to one side of the wok and make scrambled egg on the other side. Mix rice and scrambled egg well. Add chopped green onions and white pepper and stir well before serving.

CHICKEN CORDON BLEU

4 SERVINGS

4 boneless chicken breast halves, pounded to 1½ cm thickness

4 slices smoked ham

4 slices cheese

2 eggs, beaten

200 g panko bread crumbs

2 Tbsp butter, melted

1 tsp paprika powder

1 tsp garlic powder

salt and pepper

flour for dusting

Lay the chicken breast halves on a clean surface. Top each chicken breast with a slice of ham and cheese. Roll up tight, tucking ends inside.

Mix the bread crumbs with paprika powder, garlic powder, salt, pepper and melted butter. Lightly dust the chicken rolls with flour, dip each of them in egg, then roll in bread crumbs. Bake about 25 minutes until cooked through.

> **TIP**
>
> You can make the chicken cordon bleu in big batches in advance. Simply wrap each panko coated chicken breast roll in plastic wrap before storing them in the freezer.

JAPANESE-INSPIRED
CHICKEN + AVOCADO SALAD BENTO

This salad is my Mum's recipe. She has a soft spot for both Japanese sesame salad dressing and *chicken karaage,* or Japanese-style fried chicken. One day she decided to combine both in a bowl of fresh green salad and it resulted into something very delicious indeed! Thanks, Mum!

CHICKEN + AVOCADO SALAD

2 SERVINGS

JAPANESE FRIED CHICKEN

100 g chicken thigh fillet, cut into bite-size pieces

1½ Tbsp soy sauce

1 Tbsp sake

½ tsp sugar

½ Tbsp minced garlic

½ Tbsp grated ginger

2 Tbsp potato starch

oil for deep-frying

AVOCADO SALAD

1 small avocado, cut into small cubes

100 g mixed salad greens

10 cherry tomatoes

In a bowl, combine all the ingredients for the Japanese fried chicken, except the potato starch and oil. Marinate for 30 minutes. Coat the chicken pieces with potato starch and deep fry until golden brown.

Place the avocado cubes, salad greens and cherry tomatoes into a bento box. Top with a few pieces of Japanese fried chicken and serve with Japanese sesame salad dressing.

CONTENTS

Chicken & Avocado Salad

Japanese Sesame Dressing

Fruit

JAPANESE SESAME DRESSING

2 – 3 SERVINGS

3 Tbsp roasted white sesame seeds

3 Tbsp mayonnaise

1 tsp sugar

1 tsp mirin

2 Tbsp sesame oil

1 tsp soy sauce

½ tsp lemon juice

1 tsp vinegar

Grind the roasted sesame seeds in a food processor. Place the freshly ground sesame seeds in a bowl together with the rest of the ingredients and mix well.

TIP

For a quicker alternative, grab a bottle of commercially-produced Japanese sesame dressing at your local Japanese grocery store. Add a bit of sugar and sesame oil for a stronger taste, if desired.

BEEF RENDANG BENTO

Beef rendang is one of the more popular Indonesian dishes out there. It has wonderfully rich flavour, succulent texture and it tastes better with time! I usually like to make large quantity of beef rendang, because you can store it for a pretty long period of time. When refrigerated, it can last for over three weeks and when frozen, you can keep it for several months! Making beef rendang is pretty time consuming, but it's totally worth it, especially if you love spicy dishes! Serve with plenty of steamed rice and vegetables to balance out the spiciness of the rendang. Here I serve mine with purple rice – a combination of white rice and black rice, which is a healthier alternative to plain white rice.

CONTENTS

EASY AVOCADO SALAD

1 SERVING

½ small avocado, chopped

½ tsp lemon juice

½ Tbsp cream cheese

1 Tbsp mayonnaise

pinch red chilli flakes (optional)

Place chopped avocado in a bowl. Add the rest of the ingredients and mix well with a spoon.

BEEF RENDANG

6 SERVINGS

1 kg beef shanks, cut into large cubes

2 Tbsp cooking oil

5 kaffir lime leaves

1 Tbsp sugar, or to taste

200 ml coconut milk

300 ml water

salt, to taste

SPICE PASTE

5 garlic cloves

5 shallots

1 inch (2½ cm) ginger, sliced

1 inch (2½ cm) galangal, sliced

2 stalks lemongrass, sliced

10 chili peppers, de-seeded

½ tsp turmeric powder

½ tsp coriander powder

Add all of the spice paste ingredients to a food processor. Blend until fine.

Heat the cooking oil in a heavy-based saucepan. Add the blended spice paste and stir-fry until fragrant.

Add the beef cubes and cook until they turn lightly browned. Stir in the coconut milk and add the rest of the ingredients.

Turn down the heat to low and simmer the beef for 2 hours until the meat is tender and the liquid has evaporated.

> **TIP**
>
> Add extra water when the rendang is drying out during cooking.
>
> If you have frozen the beef rendang, thaw the rendang in the refrigerator before reheating it in the microwave – this way, it will take less time to heat and it also improves food safety.

BEEF RENDANG

ADDITIONAL RECIPES

—————— 83 ——————

RICE

Growing up, I used to think rice was boring. But as I grew older, I started to appreciate rice for its simplicity. A bowl of rice paired with a portion of protein and vegetables is just beautiful! Rice is also the staple food of Japan and an indispensable food item in Japanese-style bento boxes. If you love rice, like me, and regularly make rice-based bentos, invest in a rice cooker! It is one of the most reliable kitchen equipments there is.

There are many different types of rice, with white rice being the most popular. Unfortunately, even though white rice is delicious, it doesn't have much nutritional value. I myself prefer "purple rice" – a mixture of white rice with black rice, it tastes great and it's healthier too. Besides adding black rice, try mixing white rice with brown rice, other types of whole grains or even beans for more nutritious source of carbohydrate.

STEAMED WHITE RICE

2 SERVINGS

200 g white rice (short/medium grain)

350 ml water

Place rice in a pot and fill it with cold water. Wash the rice by swirling it with your hands. Drain and repeat 3 to 4 more times until the water is almost clear.

To cook the rice, fill the pot with 350 ml water and the washed rice. Bring it to a boil.

Reduce the heat to low and cover the pot. Let it cook for 15 minutes.

Turn off the heat and let it sit for 10 more minutes with the lid on. Remove the lid and fluff with a spoon.

STEAMED BROWN RICE

2 SERVINGS

200 g brown rice

500 ml water

½ tsp salt (optional)

Place the brown rice in a heavy bottomed pot and fill it with cold water. Wash the rice by swirling it with your hands. Drain and repeat 2 more times.

To cook the rice, fill the pot with 500 ml water, salt and the washed rice. Bring it to a boil. Reduce the heat to low and simmer until tender and most of the liquid has been absorbed, around 40 – 45 minutes. Turn off the heat and let it sit for 10 more minutes with the lid on. Remove the lid and fluff with a spoon.

PURPLE RICE

2 SERVINGS

150 g white rice (short/medium grain)

4 Tbsp black rice

350 ml water

Place white rice and black rice in a pot and fill it with cold water. Wash the rice by swirling it with your hands. Drain and repeat 2 more times. To cook the rice, fill the pot with 350 ml water and the washed rice. Bring it to a boil. Reduce the heat to low and cover the pot. Let it cook for 15 minutes. Turn off the heat and let it sit for 10 more minutes with the lid on. Remove the lid and fluff with a spoon.

STEAMED BROWN + WILD RICE

2 SERVINGS

150 g brown rice

4 Tbsp wild rice

550 ml water

Wash the brown and wild rice mixture in a pot by swirling it with your hands. Drain and repeat 2 more times. Fill the pot with 550 ml water and the washed rice and bring to a boil. Reduce the heat to low and simmer until tender, around 40 – 45 minutes. Turn off the heat and let it sit for 10 more minutes with the lid on. Remove the lid and fluff with a spoon.

TURMERIC RICE

2 SERVINGS

200 g medium grain rice

1 Tbsp vegetable oil

½ onion, chopped

1 tsp turmeric

¼ tsp ground cinnamon

¼ tsp ground lemongrass

3 cloves

250 ml chicken stock

250 ml coconut milk

salt and pepper

Heat oil in a saucepan and stir-fry the onion until fragrant. Stir in the rice, turmeric, cinnamon, lemon grass, cloves, salt and pepper, and toss to coat. Add the chicken stock and coconut milk and stir well. Bring to a boil and reduce heat to low. Cover and allow to simmer for 15 – 20 minutes or until the rice is tender.

INDONESIAN-STYLE FRIED RICE

1 SERVING

200 g chilled cooked rice,

3 Tbsp vegetable oil/margarine

2 Tbsp minced garlic

3 Tbsp minced shallots

3 red chili peppers, de-seeded & chopped

100 g boneless chicken breast, cut into bite
size pieces

2 Tbsp fish sauce

2 Tbsp oyster sauce

1 tsp shrimp paste

1 Tbsp sweet soy sauce

1 egg

3 Tbsp chopped green onions

Add oil to a well-heated pan. Sauté garlic, shallots,
shrimp paste and chili peppers until fragrant
and add chicken. Stir-fry over medium heat. Add
fish sauce and continue stirring until the chicken
turn lightly browned. Add rice and green onions.
Turn heat to high and stir briefly, breaking up any
clumps. Season with oyster sauce and sweet soy
sauce. Mix well. Slide the rice to the side and pour
the beaten egg onto the other side. Scramble the
egg and mix well with the rice.

SEAFOOD FRIED RICE

1 SERVING

200 g chilled cooked rice

3 Tbsp vegetable oil

2 Tbsp minced garlic

3 red chili peppers, de-seeded & chopped

100 g seafood (shrimps, squid, clams)

5 fish balls, sliced (optional)

10 petai beans/stinky beans (optional)

2 Tbsp fish sauce

2 Tbsp oyster sauce

1 Tbsp sweet soy sauce

3 Tbsp chopped green onions

Add oil to a well-heated pan. Sauté garlic and
chili peppers until fragrant. Add the seafood, fish
balls and petai beans. Stir-fry over medium heat.
Add fish sauce and continue stirring for 1 minute.
Add rice and green onions. Turn heat to high and
stir briefly, breaking up any clumps. Season with
oyster sauce and sweet soy sauce. Mix well.

STEAMED
WHITE RICE

STEAMED
BROWN RICE

PURPLE RICE

STEAMED
BROWN + WILD RICE

TURMERIC RICE

INDONESIAN-STYLE
FRIED RICE

SEAFOOD
FRIED RICE

PICKLES + SALADS

Balance out your bento lunch with tasty, fresh salads and refreshing pickles. They are not just healthy and delicious, they add wonderful colours and flavours to your bento too. I like to make big batches of pickles as they can be stored in the refrigerator for some time. If you have extra pickles or coleslaw, use them for sandwiches and salads or eat them together with meat-based dishes.

CARROT PICKLES
4 – 6 SERVINGS

2 large carrots, peeled & julienned

5 Tbsp apple cider vinegar

¼ tsp salt

1 tsp sugar

black pepper, to taste

In a bowl, combine all ingredients together and mix well. You can serve this right away, or keep refrigerated in a tight container for up to one week.

CUCUMBER + OLIVE SALAD
4 SERVINGS

1 medium cucumber

10 black olives

2 Tbsp chopped red onion

2 Tbsp olive oil

2 Tbsp balsamic vinegar

1 Tbsp lemon juice

½ tsp sugar

2 spring onions, finely sliced

½ tsp dried oregano

shredded cheddar cheese

carrot flowers, for garnish

lettuce, for garnish

Slice cucumber lengthwise into quarters and cut into small pieces. Put them into a mixing bowl and add the remaining ingredients. Toss well to combine. Garnish with shredded cheddar cheese and carrot flowers.

CRAB + CABBAGE SALAD
4 – 6 SERVINGS

6 crab sticks

2 large cabbage leaves, shredded

1 tsp apple cider vinegar

6 Tbsp Japanese mayonnaise

1 Tbsp Dijon mustard

black pepper, to taste

Shred the crab sticks by hand and combine with the shredded cabbage in a large bowl. Add the rest of the ingredients and mix well to combine and taste for seasoning. Refrigerate until ready to use, up to 2 days.

VEGETARIAN PASTA SALAD
2 SERVINGS

100 g dried rotini pasta

1 hard-boiled boiled egg, chopped

4 Tbsp frozen mixed vegetables, steamed

1 tsp chopped onion

4 Tbsp mayonnaise

1 tsp sour cream

1 tsp chopped fresh tarragon

¼ tsp sugar (optional)

salt and pepper, to taste

Cook the pasta according to the package directions. Rinse and drain.

In a bowl, toss the pasta, egg, mixed vegetables and onion with mayonnaise, sour cream and tarragon. Season with sugar, salt and pepper. Mix well.

CUCUMBER PICKLES
4 – 6 SERVINGS

2 medium English cucumbers, thinly sliced

5 Tbsp vinegar

¼ tsp salt

1 tsp sugar

black pepper, to taste

Place the cucumber slices into a bowl. Add the rest of the ingredients and mix everything together. Just like the carrot pickles, you can eat them right away, but they will taste better the next day.

EASY CABBAGE KIMCHI
10 - 15 SERVINGS

½ Chinese cabbage, cut into bite size pieces

1 L water

8 Tbsp salt

¼ pear, puréed

½ apple, puréed

1½ Tbsp sugar

100 g gochugaru

3 Tbsp fish sauce

½ onion, minced

4 Tbsp minced garlic

½ Tbsp minced ginger

Mix salt and water in a large bowl. Add the cabbage and let rest for 1½ hours. Rinse the cabbage under cold water, drain and set aside. Combine the remaining ingredients in a bowl to make the sauce. Add sauce to the cabbage and mix well. Pack kimchi in an airtight container and let it sit at room temperature for 24 hours to ferment. Refrigerate for up to 3 months.

SESAME CARROT SALAD
1 SERVING

½ carrot, peeled and julienned

1 Tbsp chopped green onion

2 Tbsp sesame oil

1 tsp apple cider vinegar

sugar and pepper, to taste

Mix all ingredients and chill before serving. Make this salad in advance and store in the refrigerator to save some preparation time.

CHERRY TOMATO + QUAIL EGG SALAD
2 SERVINGS

6 cherry tomatoes, halved

4 boiled quail eggs, peeled & halved

2 radishes, thinly sliced

salad greens

1 Tbsp chopped onion

¼ apple, peeled & chopped

½ tsp dried mixed herbs

½ tsp chicken stock powder

2 Tbsp olive oil

black pepper, to taste

croutons

In a large bowl, combine all ingredients together and mix well.

SEAFOOD + VERMICELLI SALAD
4 SERVINGS

100 g dried rice vermicelli

50 g boiled shrimps, halved

50 g boiled squid, thinly sliced

2 Tbsp tobiko, optional

2 hard-boiled eggs, peeled & chopped

1 Tbsp chopped onion

1 Tbsp lemon juice

5 Tbsp mayonnaise

½ tsp sugar

pinch pepper

Place vermicelli in a large bowl and soak in boiling water for about 3 minutes. Drain and combine with the remaining ingredients.

MASHED PURPLE POTATO SALAD
1 SERVING

½ small purple potato, peeled

1 Tbsp mayonnaise

1 Tbsp Greek yoghurt

½ tsp dried oregano

salt and pepper, to taste

Dice the purple potato and steam for 15 minutes until cooked through. Use potato masher or a spoon to mash the potato cubes until smooth. Add mayonnaise, Greek yoghurt, oregano, salt and pepper. Mix well and form into a ball with a spoon if desired.

SIMPLE ROCKET SALAD
1 SERVING

30 g rocket leaves

3 cherry tomatoes, halved

1 mini sweet pepper, de-seeded & sliced thinly

3 mini bocconcini

1 Tbsp chopped green onions

½ tsp dried mixed herbs

1 Tbsp olive oil

black pepper, to taste

Arrange the vegetables neatly as pictured (page 88). Drizzle with olive oil and sprinkle with dried mixed herbs and ground black pepper. Garnish with hard-boiled egg if desired.

BOCCONCINI SALAD
2 SERVINGS

50 g salad greens

2 medium tomatoes

10 mini bocconcini

1 Tbsp chopped basil leaves

3 Tbsp olive oil

2 Tbsp balsamic vinegar

black pepper, to taste

2 cherry tomatoes, for garnish

carrot flowers, for garnish

Slice the tomatoes thinly. Mix them with the salad greens. Add the mini bocconcini balls and chopped basil leaves.

Drizzle with olive oil and balsamic vinegar and sprinkle with black pepper to taste. Garnish with cherry tomatoes and carrot flowers

COLESLAW
4 – 6 SERVINGS

3 cabbage leaves, finely shredded

1 carrot, finely shredded

5 Tbsp mayonnaise

1 Tbsp sour cream

1 tsp grated onion

1 tsp mustard

1 tsp vinegar

1 tsp sugar, or to taste

salt and pepper, to taste

Combine all the ingredients in a large bowl and mix well. This homemade coleslaw can be stored in the refrigerator for up to 5 days.

CRAB + CABBAGE
SALAD

VEGETARIAN
PASTA SALAD

CARROT
PICKLES

CUCUMBER
PICKLES

EASY
CABBAGE KIMCHI

SESAME
CARROT SALAD

CHERRY TOMATO + QUAIL EGG
SALAD

SEAFOOD + VERMICELLI
SALAD

MASHED
PURPLE POTATO SALAD

SIMPLE
ROCKET SALAD

CUCUMBER + OLIVE
SALAD

BOCCONCINI
SALAD

COLESLAW

STIR FRIES + OTHER FAVOURITES

Stir-frying is a quick, versatile and healthy cooking technique. It is also a great way to use leftovers. You don't need much cooking oil to make a good stir-fry, I usually just use around one tablespoon oil, depending on the amount of meat and vegetables that I cook. I have included some stir-fry recipes and other favourites of mine, which also work well as bento fillers.

STIR-FRIED STRING BEANS WITH SHRIMPS

2 – 3 SERVINGS

250 g string beans, cut into 4 cm pieces

1 tsp minced garlic

100 g shrimps, shelled & de-veined

1 Tbsp oyster sauce

1 Tbsp Shaoxing wine

1 Tbsp fish sauce

½ tsp sugar

pinch white pepper

1 Tbsp cooking oil

Sauté the minced garlic until fragrant. Add shrimps and stir- fry for 20 seconds until the shrimps are about to turn pink. Add the string beans, Shaoxing wine, fish sauce, oyster sauce and sugar. Toss to combine and cook for another 2 – 3 minutes. Turn off the heat and sprinkle with a pinch of white pepper.

BEEFSTEAK WITH WHITE WINE TERIYAKI SAUCE

1 SERVING

150 g beefsteak, cut into bite-size pieces

5 Tbsp white wine

4 Tbsp soy sauce

1 tsp sugar

1 Tbsp chopped green onion

pinch black pepper

oil for pan-frying

Toss in beef cubes and stir-fry until the beef is slightly brown. Add white wine and mix well.

Add soy sauce, sugar and pepper and cook the beef until the sauce thickens. Garnish with chopped green onion.

TURKEY WITH BLACK BEAN SAUCE

1 SERVING

120 g turkey breast, cut into bite-sized pieces

8 string beans, cut into 4 cm lengths

½ Tbsp minced garlic

1 Tbsp oyster sauce

1 Tbsp spicy black bean sauce

2 bird's eye chili peppers, de-seeded & chopped

sugar and pepper, to taste

oil for pan-frying

Heat the oil in a frying pan over medium heat. Add the garlic and chopped bird's eye chili peppers. Cook until fragrant, about 20 seconds. Add the turkey and stir-fry until it is cooked through. Add the string beans and drizzle with oyster sauce and black bean sauce. Season with sugar and pepper.

SIMPLE TOMATO SPAGHETTI

1 – 2 SERVINGS

100 g dried spaghetti

2 Tbsp olive oil

1 Tbsp minced garlic

2 Tbsp tomato paste

1 Tbsp heavy cream

½ tsp dried basil

grated Parmesan cheese, to taste

salt and pepper, to taste

Boil spaghetti according to package directions until al dente. Set aside.

Coat a well heated pan with olive oil. Add minced garlic and stir-fry until fragrant. Add tomato paste, cream and dried basil. Season with salt and pepper.

Transfer spaghetti into the sauce and stir well. Add grated Parmesan cheese to taste.

BAKED CHICKEN NUGGETS

6 – 8 SERVINGS

500 g boneless chicken breast, cut into 5 cm pieces

1 tsp ground paprika

1 tsp garlic powder

1 tsp chicken stock powder

½ tsp dried mixed herbs

2 Tbsp grated Parmesan cheese

salt and pepper

200 g breadcrumbs

100 g flour

2 eggs, beaten

olive oil cooking spray

Preheat oven to 200°C.

In a bowl, mix the chicken pieces together with paprika, garlic powder, chicken powder, dried mixed herbs, Parmesan cheese, salt and pepper.

Set the eggs, flour and bread crumbs in three different shallow bowls. One at a time, dredge the chicken pieces in the flour, then dip in egg and coat with the bread crumbs.

Spray chicken with oil and bake for 15 minutes.

MISO CHICKEN ROLLS

1 – 2 SERVINGS

150 g chicken thigh fillet

2 Tbsp sake

1 Tbsp soy sauce

1 tsp minced ginger

1 Tbsp miso

1 tsp sugar

pinch black pepper

Trim the chicken and flatten to ½ cm thickness. Combine the remaining ingredients and rub onto the chicken. Marinate 20 – 30 minutes.

Roll up the fillet and tuck in ends; secure with toothpicks. Broil or grill until golden brown and done inside. Remove toothpicks and slice.

STIR-FRIED STRING
BEANS WITH SHRIMPS

BEEF WITH WHITE WINE
TERIYAKI SAUCE

TURKEY WITH BLACK
BEAN SAUCE

SIMPLE
TOMATO SPAGHETTI

BAKED
CHICKEN NUGGETS

MISO
CHICKEN ROLLS

VEGETABLE + HAM ROLLS

MAKES 8

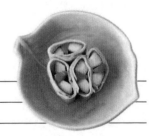

4 slices smoked ham

¼ carrot, cut into strips

¼ cucumber, cut into strips

Lay one slice of ham on a cutting board. Place 2 strips of cucumber and 1 strip of carrot about 1 cm from the edge of the ham. Roll tightly. Cut the roll into two equal pieces. Repeat with the rest of the ingredients.

GROUND BEEF + BROCCOLI STIR-FRY

2 – 4 SERVINGS

½ head broccoli

100 g ground pork

6 button mushrooms, halved

¼ small onion, thinly sliced

1 Tbsp minced garlic

2 Tbsp vegetable oil

1 Tbsp fish sauce

2 Tbsp oyster sauce

2 red chili peppers, de-seeded & sliced

sugar and pepper, to taste

Add vegetable oil to a well-heated pan. Sauté garlic, chili peppers, onion and ground pork until lightly browned and aromatic. Add mushrooms, broccoli and fish sauce. Quickly stir-fry for a few seconds before adding the rest of the ingredients. Stir and coat.

SPICY STRING BEANS

4 SERVINGS

400 g string beans

100 g ground pork or chicken

2 Tbsp cooking oil

1 Tbsp minced garlic

1 tsp minced ginger

3 bird's eye chili peppers, de-seeded & chopped

2 Tbsp fish sauce

1½ Tbsp oyster sauce

sugar, to taste

pinch black pepper

Heat cooking oil in wok over high heat: Stir in ginger, chopped chili peppers and garlic until fragrant. Add ground pork and cook until the meat begins to turn brown. Add the green beans, fish sauce, oyster sauce, sugar and black pepper and stir well. Cover and cook over medium-low heat, stirring occasionally, until the beans are crisp-tender.

SIMPLIFIED SWEET + SOUR PORK

4 – 6 SERVINGS

400 g pork tenderlion, cut into bite size pieces

1 Tbsp minced garlic

1 Tbsp soy sauce

½ tsp corn starch

BATTER

5 Tbsp flour

5 Tbsp corn flour

½ tsp baking soda

5 Tbsp water

1 egg white, lightly beaten

SWEET & SOUR SAUCE

2 Tbsp ketchup

2 Tbsp soy sauce

1 Tbsp vinegar

1 Tbsp oyster sauce

5 Tbsp pineapple juice

1 tsp corn starch

1 tsp sugar, or to taste

Mix the pork with 1 tablespoon minced garlic, 1 tablespoon soy sauce and ½ teaspoon corn starch. Marinate for 30 minutes.

To prepare the sauce, combine all the ingredients in a bowl and mix well. Set aside.

Mix all of the batter ingredients together in a bowl. Transfer the marinated pork pieces into the batter to coat. Deep fry the pork until golden brown. Remove and drain on paper towels.

Bring the sweet and sour sauce to a boil. When the sauce thickens, add the pork pieces and toss to coat.

SPICY PORK BULGOGI

2 – 4 SERVINGS

200 g pork butt or shoulder, thinly sliced

MARINADE

2 Tbsp gochujang

1 tsp gochugaru

1 tsp sugar

2 Tbsp soy sauce

2 Tbsp dry sherry

1 Tbsp sesame oil

½ onion, thinly sliced

1 Tbsp minced garlic

½ apple or pear, puréed

2 scallions, chopped

Combine pork with the marinade ingredients. Mix well and leave to marinate for 30 minutes (or even better, overnight).

Grill or stir-fry the pork for around 3 minutes. Add some more onion slices and roasted sesame seeds if desired and cook for another minute.

SAVOURY TOFU STIR-FRY

2 SERVINGS

1 block regular tofu, diced

6 shiitake mushrooms, thinly sliced

1 Tbsp vegetable oil

½ Tbsp minced garlic

½ tsp minced ginger

1 Tbsp fish sauce

1 Tbsp oyster sauce

1 Tbsp sesame oil

salt, pepper & sugar, to taste

1 tsp corn flour, dissolved in 2 Tbsp water

Add vegetable oil to a well-heated pan and sauté garlic and ginger over medium heat. Add tofu, mushrooms and fish sauce and stir-fry for 1 minute. Season with oyster sauce, sesame oil, salt, pepper and sugar to taste. Pour the corn starch/water mixture and stir until the sauce thickens.

COCONUT CHICKEN

2 SERVINGS

200 g boneless chicken breast, cut into bite size pieces

2 Tbsp vegetable oil

1 Tbsp minced garlic

½ tsp ground cinnamon

½ tsp ground cumin

½ tsp ground coriander

½ tsp ground turmeric

1 tsp sambal oelek (chili paste)

2 Tbsp sweet soy sauce

1 Tbsp fish sauce

200 ml coconut milk

salt and pepper, to taste

Add vegetable oil to a well-heated pan and sauté garlic and chicken until lightly browned. Add the rest of the ingredients and cook until the chicken is tender.

SWEET PEPPER CHICKEN STIR-FRY

2 – 4 SERVINGS

200 g boneless chicken, cut into bite size pieces

1 sweet pepper, de-seeded & diced

1 Tbsp chopped onion

6 button mushrooms, sliced

1 Tbsp sesame oil

1 Tbsp soy sauce

1 Tbsp oyster sauce

2 Tbsp white wine

pinch salt and pepper

Add sesame oil to a well-heated pan. Add onion and chicken, and season with salt and pepper. Sauté over medium high. When the chicken turns brown, add mushrooms, diced sweet peppers, cooking wine, soy sauce and oyster sauce. Stir-fry and cook for another minute.

STEAMED CHICKEN + VEGETABLE MEATBALLS

MAKES 16 -20

400 g ground chicken

½ carrot, peeled & chopped

6 string beans, chopped

2 scallions, chopped

1 Tbsp grated onion

1 Tbsp oysters sauce

1 Tbsp sesame oil

¼ tsp sugar

1 tsp chicken stock powder

2 Tbsp corn starch

pinch white pepper

Combine ground chicken with all the other ingredients. Form golf-sized meatballs with wet hands. Steam the meatballs for 15 minutes or until cooked through.

PRAWN CAKES

4 SERVINGS

400 g raw prawn meat, finely chopped

1 Tbsp minced onion

1 tsp minced garlic

3 Tbsp chopped carrot

2 Tbsp chopped green onion

1 egg, beaten

3 Tbsp corn flour

3 Tbsp bread crumbs

1 Tbsp oyster sauce

1 Tbsp fish sauce

sugar and pepper, to taste

pinch black pepper

Put all the ingredients into a bowl and mix well. Divide the mixture into equal portions and shape into patties. Pan-fry the prawn cakes until cooked through and golden brown.

FRIED SHRIMP BALLS

MAKES 15 - 20 BALLS

15 – 20 slices white bread – remove the brown sides and cut into small cubes

500 grams shrimps, finely chopped

2 green onions, chopped

1 egg

1 ½ Tbsp oyster sauce

1 Tbsp fish sauce

white pepper, to taste

½ tsp baking soda

5 Tbsp corn flour

Mix all the ingredients in a bowl, except the white bread cubes. Take one tablespoon of the shrimp mixture and coat it with the bread cubes. Shape the bread coated shrimp mixture into a ball. Repeat. Deep fry the shrimp balls until golden brown.

SHRIMP + VEGETABLE FRITTERS

4 SERVINGS

½ onion, thinly sliced

½ small carrot, julienned

1 spring onion, chopped

10 shrimps, shelled & de-veined

1 Tbsp oyster sauce

pinch white pepper

5 Tbsp all-purpose flour

6 Tbsp ice water

1 egg yolk

oil for deep frying

Combine the flour, egg yolk and ice water to form the batter. Add the remaining ingredients in the batter and mix well.

Heat oil in a pan over medium heat. Take a scoop of the mixture with a spatula and gently slide into the oil. Shape each fritter with chopsticks. Fry until crisp and golden brown.

VEGETABLE + BEEF ROLLS

2 – 4 SERVINGS

4 thinly sliced beef tenderloin

8 blanched string beans

½ blanched carrot, cut into strips

2 Tbsp flour

pinch salt and pepper

1 Tbsp vegetable oil

SAUCE

2 Tbsp soy sauce

1 Tbsp sake

1 Tbsp mirin

1 tsp sugar

½ tsp dashi powder

2 Tbsp water

Place a slice of beef on a cutting board. Sprinkle with flour, salt and pepper. Lay two pieces each of string beans and carrot strips on one side of the beef slice and roll up tightly. Dust the beef rolls lightly with flour and set aside. Repeat with the rest of the beef slices. Heat the vegetable oil in a pan and cook the beef rolls until both sides are nicely browned.

Combine soy sauce, sake, mirin, sugar, dashi powder and water in a bowl. Pour the sauce to the pan and turn the beef rolls to coat. Reduce heat to a simmer and cook beef until the sauce has thickened and almost evaporated. Remove the beef rolls and cut in half before serving.

SIMMERED BLACK BEANS

4 SERVINGS

100 g black beans

700 ml water

2 Tbsp soy sauce

1 Tbsp dashi powder

1 Tbsp sugar

Rinse the black beans and place in a deep pot. Pour 700 ml water and let the beans soak overnight.

Turn the stove on to medium-high heat. Bring the beans to a boil. Reduce the heat to low and let the black beans simmer for 4 – 5 hours or until the beans are tender, adding water if necessary. Season with soy sauce, dashi powder and sugar. Mix well.

PAN-FRIED WONTONS

MAKES 50

300 g ground pork

150 g chopped shrimps

1 egg white

3 Tbsp oyster sauce

2 Tbsp fish sauce

1 Tbsp minced garlic

1 tsp grated ginger

4 scallions, chopped

¼ tsp sugar

pinch pepper

50 wonton wrappers

Combine all of the ingredients, except the wonton wrappers, in a bowl and mix well.

Place 1 teaspoon of wonton filling onto the centre of each wrapper. Fold the wrapper in half, pleat and seal with water.

Pan-fry the wontons until cooked through and golden brown.

SPICY RICE CAKES

2 SERVINGS

20 frozen Korean cylindrical rice cakes

1 Tbsp vegetable oil

1 tsp minced garlic

50 g ground pork

1 Tbsp gochujang

½ tsp gochugaru

1 Tbsp fish sauce

1 Tbsp oyster sauce

1 tsp dashi powder

1 tsp sesame oil

100 ml water

½ tsp sugar

extra water, for boiling rice cakes

Cook the rice cakes in boiling water for 2 minutes. Drain and set aside.

Sauté garlic and ground pork until lightly browned. Add the rice cakes and the rest of the ingredients and bring to a boil. Cook for an additional 2 minutes or until the sauce has thickened.

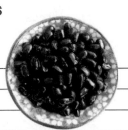

BULGUR PILAF

2 – 3 SERVINGS

250 g bulgur

500 ml water

1 Tbsp minced garlic

1 large onion, sliced

4 dried chillies

2 sweet peppers, seeded & sliced thinly

10 string beans, cut into 5 cm pieces

200 g chicken breast, cut into cubes

1 Tbsp olive oil

2 Tbsp tomato paste

chicken stock powder to taste

a pinch of ground paprika, garlic powder

and ground cumin

Heat oil in a skillet. Sauté garlic, onion and dried chillies until fragrant. Add the chicken and cook until lightly browned.

Add bulgur, chicken stock powder, cumin, paprika and garlic powder, and toss to coat.

Pour water and add tomato paste. Bring to a boil, stir, cover and simmer over medium-low heat until all liquid is absorbed and the bulgur is cooked.

In a separate skillet, stir-fry the sweet peppers and string beans for about 1 to 2 minutes. Season with salt and pepper. Quickly toss into the bulgur and mix well.

SIMMERED POTATOES

1 – 2 SERVINGS

1 potato, peeled & cut into small chunks

1 Tbsp vegetable oil

1 Tbsp chopped onion

1 Tbsp soy sauce

1 Tbsp sake

½ tsp dashi powder

1 tsp sugar

100 ml water

Heat oil in a well-heated pan and sauté onion until lightly browned. Add the potato chunks, soy sauce, sake, dashi powder, water and sugar. Cook until the sauce has evaporated and the potatoes are tender, adding extra water if necessary.

SOY SAUCE EGGS

4 – 6 SERVINGS

4 eggs (room temperature)

1 L water

soy sauce

Bring water to a full boil in a saucepan. Place the eggs gently into the saucepan with a spoon. Make sure that the eggs are completely covered in water. Cook for 7 minutes. Remove the eggs and place them in a bowl of cold water to stop the cooking process. Peel the eggs carefully after they have cooled down.

Pour soy sauce into a zip lock bag and place the peeled eggs inside to marinate for 1 hour. The longer you let the eggs sit in soy sauce, the darker and saltier the eggs will be.

TEA EGGS

4 SERVINGS

4 medium eggs

800 ml water

5 Tbsp soy sauce

1 Tbsp sugar

2 teabags black tea

½ tsp cinnamon powder

½ tsp five-spice powder

Bring water to a full boil in a saucepan. Cook the eggs for 8 minutes. Remove the eggs and crack the eggshells with a spoon gently. Place the cracked eggs back into the saucepan. Add the remaining ingredients and bring to a boil. Turn off the heat and leave the eggs in the tea mixture overnight. Peel the eggs before serving.

TAMAGOYAKI

Tamagoyaki is such a popular bento item, I decided it deserves its own special page in this book! I think everybody who is into Japanese bento boxes knows what tamagoyaki is. It refers to Japanese-style rolled omelette. Tamagoyaki is also a popular sushi topping. You might have seen it at your local sushi bar. To make tamagoyaki yourself at home, a rectangular tamagoyaki pan is not necessary. A non-stick round skillet will do just fine. I also like my tamagoyaki savoury, so I don't include sugar in my tamagoyaki, but feel free to add sugar to your tamagoyaki as desired.

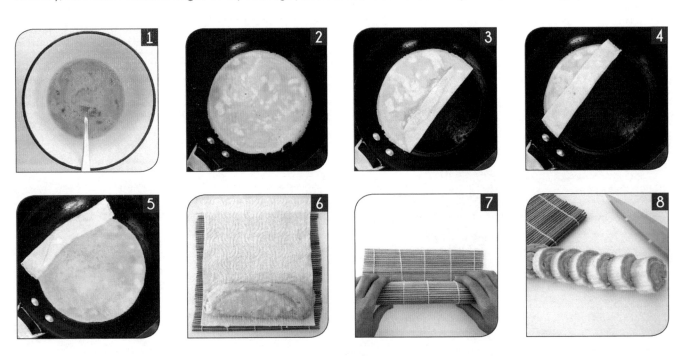

BASIC TAMAGOYAKI

2 SERVINGS

3 eggs

1 tsp mirin

½ tsp dashi powder

¼ tsp sugar (optional)

oil for frying

Combine the egg, mirin and dashi powder in a bowl (see 1).

Heat oil in a non-stick pan over medium heat. Pour a thin layer of the egg mixture into the pan (see 2). When half done, roll the egg to one side of the pan (see 3 – 4). Brush the empty side of the pan with oil and pour another thin layer of egg mixture in the space and under the rolled egg (see 5).

Repeat steps 3 – 5 until the egg mixture is all used up.

Flip the egg out onto a paper towel to soak up any excess oil (see 6). To make a cylindrical tamagoyaki, roll a bamboo mat around the tamagoyaki and squeeze firmly like rolling a sushi roll (see 7). Cool and cut into slices (see 8).

GREEN ONION TAMAGOYAKI

2 SERVINGS

1 Tbsp chopped green onion

pinch black pepper

Add the green onion and a pinch of pepper to the basic tamagoyaki egg mixture, and follow Steps 2 – 8.

CRAB TAMAGOYAKI

2 SERVINGS

100 g crab meat, shredded

1 Tbsp chopped green onion

1 tsp soy sauce

pinch black pepper

Add the crab meat, green onion and a pinch of pepper to the basic tamagoyaki egg mixture, and follow Steps 2 – 8.

HAM + CHEESE + CARROT TAMAGOYAKI

2 SERVINGS

2 slices smoked ham, chopped

1 slice cheddar cheese, chopped

1 Tbsp chopped carrot

1 Tbsp chopped green onion

½ tsp soy sauce

pinch black pepper

Add all of the above ingredients to the basic tamagoyaki egg mixture, and follow Steps 2 – 8.

TOMATO + CHEESE + GREEN ONION TAMAGOYAKI

2 SERVINGS

1 medium tomato, thinly sliced

1 Tbsp chopped green onion

1 Tbsp shredded cheese

pinch black pepper

Add the green onion, tomato slices, cheese and pepper to the basic tamagoyaki egg mixture, and follow Steps 2 – 8.

> **TIP**
>
> If you notice that your tamagoyaki is a bit runny, microwave it for 30 seconds – 1 minute, it's going to firm it up.

FURTHER TIPS + TRICKS

ONIGIRI

Onigiri is a rice ball commonly shaped into triangles, discs or cylinders and is often wrapped in roasted seaweed. It is a Japanese comfort food, which can easily be found in convenience stores, supermarkets and even vending machines in Japan. The most basic type of onigiri is made with plain white rice and a bit of salt. However, more popular onigiri are usually filled with savoury ingredients, such as pickled plums, salted salmon or fried shrimps. Onigiri can also be formed into various fun shapes, like a rabbit or a bear.

To make onigiri, use short or medium grain rice. Make sure that the rice is warm, since cold rice doesn't stick together very well. Traditionally, people in Japan wet their palms with salted water before forming onigiri into different shapes, to prevent rice from sticking to their hands. I myself prefer to mould onigiri with plastic wrap. I just find this method quicker, easier and cleaner. Basically this is what you do – place a scoop of warm rice in the centre of a plastic wrap. If you want to fill the onigiri, place your desired filling on top of the rice. Cover the filling with about one tablespoon of rice, and gather up the ends of the plastic wrap before twisting it tightly to form a ball. If you want to shape the onigiri differently, keep the rice ball in the plastic wrap and squeeze it with your palms into other shapes of your choice.

Below you will find some examples of traditional and not so traditional onigiri fillings. You can nevertheless fill an onigiri with anything you like and wrap it with other things than seaweed. Make your own unique onigiri combinations and have fun!

TRIANGLE

DISC

CYLINDER

TRADITIONAL	NON-TRADITIONAL
pickled plums	fried chicken
salted salmon	shrimp tempura
bonito flakes + soy sauce	chicken teriyaki
japanese pickles	meatballs
miso + green onions	western pickles
spicy pollock roe	tuna + mayonnaise
salted pollock roe	kimchi +ham
marinated salmon roe	shrimps + mayonnaise
konbu seaweed	smoked salmon + cream cheese
raw tuna	beef bulgogi
raw salmon roe	chicken curry

TIP

Make a big batch of onigiri, wrap each of them with a plastic wrap and freeze them for later use. Simply defrost the onigiri at room temperature before consuming.

COLOURING RICE

If you are into *charaben*, it is very likely that you will want to know how to colour rice using natural ingredients. Creating characters with plain white rice is boring, unless the characters you intend to make are meant to be white. There are quite a lot of natural dyes which are suitable to colour rice, usually extracted from different types of vegetables and spices. Below are just a few examples of ingredients, which can be used to dye rice. I have also listed a couple more examples of food items that are great for colouring rice and even eggs on page 103.

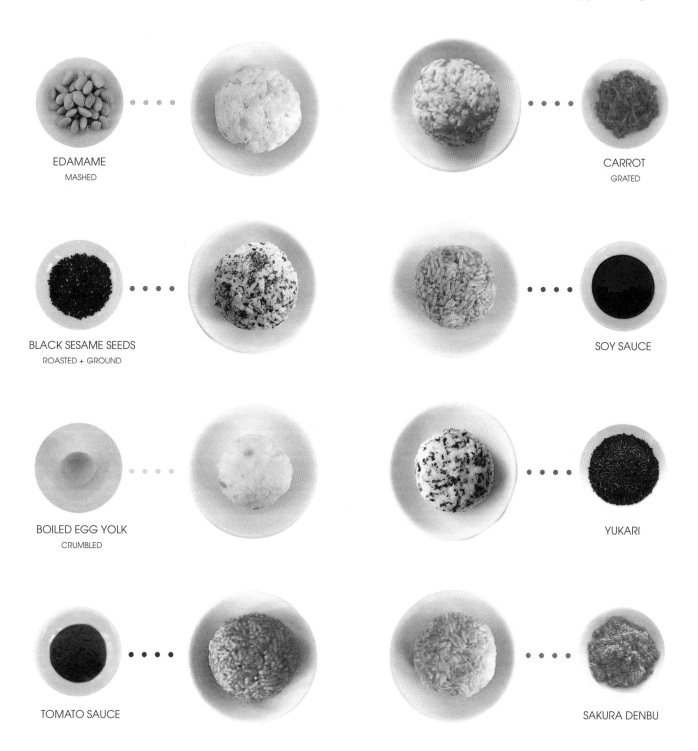

EDAMAME
MASHED

CARROT
GRATED

BLACK SESAME SEEDS
ROASTED + GROUND

SOY SAUCE

BOILED EGG YOLK
CRUMBLED

YUKARI

TOMATO SAUCE

SAKURA DENBU

BENTO HELPERS

These items below are store-bought pickles and sprinkles which I find useful for bento making. All of them are fantastic additions to bento – not only are they delicious, they keep well and they add some colours to your packed lunch too! Keep a variety of preserved foods on hand and remember that they don't have to be Japanese!

Japanese rice sprinkles, such as yukari and sakura denbu, are also ideal for colouring rice besides adding flavour to plain rice. For instance, if you want to make pink rice, but you can't be bothered to make some beetroot juice (see page 33), sakura denbu is a quick and easy solution! The drawback is, if you are not into fish, you might find the smell of sakura denbu rather unpleasant and somewhat off-putting.

SHIBAZUKE
PICKLED CUCUMBER + EGGPLANT

PICKLED GHERKINS

BENI SHOGA
PICKLED GINGER

TAKUAN
PICKLED DAIKON

UMEBOSHI
PICKLED PLUM (CRUNCHY)

UMEBOSHI
PICKLED PLUM (SOFT)

FUKUJINZUKE
PICKLED RADISH + VEGETABLE

CHOPPED CUCUMBER PICKLES

SAKURA DENBU
DRIED + GROUND SEASONED CODFISH

YUKARI
DRIED RED PERILLA LEAVES

IDEA LIST FOR A COLOURFUL BENTO BOX

People who are familiar with my bento style know that my bento lunches tend to be very bright and colourful. You can achieve this easily by including several food items in various colours into your bento box. Vegetables and fruit are excellent natural colourful foods, which are not just healthy and nutritious, but lovely to look at too.

I like big portions of fruit, however a lot of fruits tend to be high in sugar, so feel free to reduce the portion as you wish! I also like to colour and form rice into fun shapes, as you can see yourself in the Character Bento section of this book. Colouring hard-boiled eggs and transforming them into cute characters is another trick that I like to use to prettify my bento (see page 33 for example). Please find the marked ingredients below for a list of food items that I sometimes use to colour rice (*) and dye eggs (•).

aonori *	cucumber	lettuce
asparagus	edamame *	parsley
avocado	green grapes	peas *
bok choy *	green onions	spinach *
broccoli *	kale *	string beans
celery	kiwi	honeydew

apple	raspberries
chili sauce *	red pepper
crabstick	salami
fukujinzuke	strawberries
gochujang *	tomatoes
pickled plum	tomato sauce *
radish	watermelon

banana
boiled egg yolk *
cheese
corn
curry powder • *
mango
pasta
pineapple
saffron • *
takuan
turmeric • *

blackberries
black beans
black sesame seeds *
caviar
nori seaweed

black rice
purple potatoes *
purple carrot *
red cabbage juice • *
shibazuke
yukari *

purple potato powder *
purple carrot juice • *
red cabbage juice + baking soda • *
shibazuke pickling liquid • *

bocconcini
cauliflower
feta cheese
goat cheese
turkey cold cuts
white rice

carrot *
clementine
orange sweet pepper
papaya
pumpkin *

beetroot juice • *	red cabbage
boiled shrimps	liquid + vinegar •
ham	sakura denbu *

almond	fried tofu	pretzels
brown rice	katsuoboshi *	soba noodles
fried meatballs	pork floss *	soy sauce • *

PRETTY BENTO ACCENTS

I love adding lovely, edible ornaments in my bento. This is what makes a regular packed lunch a bento in my opinion. Of course the word bento itself simply means a portable lunch in a box, and little frills and embellishments are not necessary – not everyone in Japan decorate their bento lunches and I don't always add whimsical cutouts as garnish either. You can still make beautiful and appealing bento meals by arranging food neatly and by using the natural, vibrant colours and textures of various food items. However, decorative bento accents are fun and I have a personal preference for anything pretty – so I just can't help myself not to include some neat elements in my bento box! After all, cutting a carrot into little strips and cutting out a carrot flower with a cookie cutter doesn't make much difference practically. Try to make some of the following bento accents for special occasions, it's not as complicated as it seems!

CHEESE FLOWERS

Making cheese flowers or cutting other fun shapes out of cheese is very easy if you have some cookie or vegetable cutters at home.

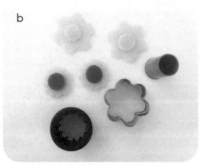

Top the cheese flowers with vegetable or deli meat cutouts to make the cheese flowers more decorative and attractive.

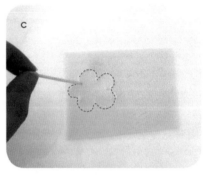

If you don't have any cookie cutters, it is also possible to hand cut the shapes yourself using the help of a toothpick.

CARROT FLOWERS

Slice carrot thinly and cut out flower shapes with flower cutters.

Punch out little stars or circles in the middle of the carrot flowers for more sophisticated-looking flowers.

Try other shapes, such as butterflies, teddy bears or rabbits and have lots of fun!

HAM ROSES

Halve 3 slices of smoked ham – you will end up with 6 halved-slices, which will make the rose petals.

Take one of the halved slices and roll it up. This will be the centre bud.

Take another halved slice of ham and wrap it around the centre bud from step b.

Repeat step c with the remaining slices of ham and you will end up with a rose! Secure the ham rose with a small piece of spaghetti.

DELI MEAT FLOWERS

You will need a slice of firm-textured deli meat for optimal result. Cut the slice of deli meat in half.

Take one half of the deli meat slice, and cut lines in the middle of it, but not all the way.

Fold the deli meat in half.

Roll it up.

Keep rolling and make sure to roll tightly to keep it together.

Use an uncooked spaghetti noodle stick to secure the end, or tie with green onion.

CUCUMBER "LEAVES"

Use a kitchen knife to slice the skin of a cucumber lengthwise, about 1 cm thick and 4 cm wide. Use a decorative cookie cutter (i.e. leaf) to cut the cucumber into leaves. To carve the cucumber leaf, make a curved incision (right to left) vertically in the middle of the leaf with your knife. Now cut towards the incision you already made and this time from left to right, making a V wedge. Remove the wedge. Now repeat exactly the same steps as before, but this time you make the incisions on the right and left parts of the leaf.

EGG TULIPS

To make the egg tulips, you will need peeled hard-boiled eggs. Take one of the eggs and make zigzag cuts around the middle of the egg with a small, sharp knife. Gently pull the egg halves apart. Repeat with the rest of the hard-boiled eggs. To make sure that each egg tulip stands up straight, cut a thin slice from the rounded bottom of each egg half.

You can also season the egg yolk à la devilled egg if you wish. Carefully scoop out the yolk and place in a small mixing bowl. Using a fork, mash the yolk until fine. Mix in ½ tablespoon mayonnaise, ½ teaspoon Dijon mustard, garlic powder and pepper to taste. Fill each of the hollowed egg white "shells" with the seasoned egg yolk.

RESOURCE GUIDE

——— 107 ———

ONLINE RETAILERS FOR BENTO SUPPLIES

ALL THINGS FOR SALE
www.allthingsforsale.com

AMAZON
www.amazon.com

BENTO & CO
www.bentoandco.com

CASA BENTO
www.casabento.com

EBAY
www.ebay.com

ECO LUNCHBOX
www.ecolunchboxes.com

FROM JAPAN WITH LOVE
www.from-japan-with-love.com

J-BOX
www.jbox.com

JAPAN CENTRE
www.japancentre.com

LAPTOP LUNCHES
www.laptoplunches.com

MODES4U
www.modes4u.com

MON BENTO
www.monbento.com

RAKUTEN INTERNATIONAL
www.en.rakuten.co.jp

BENTO BLOGS

ADVENTURES IN BENTO MAKING
www.aibento.net

ANNA THE RED
www.annathered.com

BENTOLICIOUS
www.mybentolicious.com

BENTO ZEN
www.bentozen.wordpress.com

BOHNENHASE
www.bohnenhase.blogspot.com

BONITA FOOD
www.bonitofood.blogspot.com

COOKING CUTE
www.cookingcute.com

HAPPY LITTLE BENTO
www.happylittlebento.blogspot.com

JUST BENTO
www.justbento.com

LUNCH IN A BOX
www.lunchinabox.net

WENDOLONIA
www.wendolonia.com

ASIAN RECIPE BLOGS

AERI'S KITCHEN
www.aeriskitchen.com

EATING ASIA
www.eatingasia.typepad.com

JUST HUNGRY
www.justhungry.com

JUST ONE COOKBOOK
www.justonecookbook.com

LILY'S WAI SEK HONG
www.lilyng2000.blogspot.com

MAANGCHI'S KOREAN COOKING
www.maangchi.com

NO RECIPES
www.norecipes.com

RASA MALAYSIA
www.rasamalyasia.com

STEAMY KITCHEN
www.steamykitchen.com

INSPIRATIONAL COOKBOOKS

BENTO BOXES
Naomi Kijima

BENTO LOVE
Kentaro Kobayashi

CHINESE RICE + NOODLES
Su Huei Huang & Mu Tsun Lee

FACE FOOD RECIPES
Christopher D Salyers

JAPANESE CUISINE FOR EVERYONE
Yukiko Moriyama

KOREAN COOKING FOR EVERYONE
Ji Sook Choe & Yukiko Moriyama

THE JUST BENTO COOKBOOK
Makiko Itoh

YUM YUM BENTO BOX
Maki Ogawa & Crystal Watanabe

GLOSSARY

— 111 —

AONORI

Aonori refers to powdered green seaweed and is often added as a topping to some popular Japanese savoury dishes, such as takoyaki and okonomiyaki.

BARAN

Decorative food dividers – the most common are the thin plastic green grass sheets, often used to separate sushi from wasabi and pickled ginger.

BENI SHOGA

Beni shoga is another word for red pickled ginger. Usually cut into thin strips, beni shoga is often used to garnish many Japanese savoury dishes.

BLACK BEAN SAUCE

Black bean sauce is made from fermented soy beans mixed with other spices such as garlic and chili peppers. Pre-made black bean sauce is usually readily available in most Asian grocery stores.

CHARABEN

An abbreviation for Character Bento – an elaborately arranged packed lunch, which features food resembling famous people, pop culture icons, animals or whimsical shapes and cutouts.

COCONUT MILK

Coconut milk is rich and creamy fluid extracted from the flesh of a coconut fruit. Its texture makes it a good base for curry dishes. A lot of Southeast Asian desserts also use coconut milk as one of the main ingredients.

CRAB STICKS

Also known as surimi, imitation crab meat or seafood sticks, crab sticks do not contain actual crab meat and are typically made from processed white pollock fish.

DASHI

A simple Japanese soup stock, generally made by simmering konbu seaweed with katsuoboshi (dried bonito shavings). Instant dashi powders can be found at Japanese or Asian grocery stores, but a lot of them tend to contain monosodium glutamate (MSG). Look for MSG-free dashi powders – they will make a good addition to your bento pantry!

DUMPLING WRAPPERS

Dumpling wrappers or gow gee wrappers are used to make a variety of Chinese dumplings, including the Japanese and Korean variants, gyoza and mandu. Different to wonton wrappers, the dough of gow gee wrapper is only made from a mixture of wheat flour and water without the addition of egg. Commercially produced gow gee wrappers are typically white and round.

EDAMAME

Edamame are young, green soybeans, usually boiled or steamed and seasoned with salt. They are great for bento and are very healthy too. Hulled edamame beans can usually be found in the frozen section of Asian grocery stores.

FISH BALLS

Fish balls are similar to Asian-style meatballs, but use fish instead of meat as the main ingredient. Like quail eggs, white coloured fish balls are great for creating various characters' faces for character bento.

FISH FLOSS

Fish floss has a light and fluffy texture, similar to meat floss, which is a popular food item in Chinese cuisine and some Southeast Asian countries. It is made of fish that has been cooked, crumbled, seasoned and dried. Fish floss is often eaten as a snack or used as a topping for rice, bread and salad.

FISH SAUCE

Fish sauce is a translucent reddish-brown liquid made from a mixture of fish, water and salt. It is a staple condiment and seasoning in some Asian countries, especially in Vietnam, Thailand and Cambodia. Fish sauce makes great seasoning for stir-fries, soups and dipping sauces.

FUKUJINZUKE

Pickled in soy sauce and mirin, this crunchy Japanese pickle is commonly served as garnish to Japanese curry and rice. The most common ingredients for fukujinzuke are daikon (Japanese radish), cucumber, eggplant and lotus root.

GALANGAL

Galangal is a type of ginger. It can be distinguished by its reddish-brown skin and its resemblance to ginger. Fresh galangal is very aromatic and can be purchased at the fresh or frozen section of Asian grocery stores.

HOT CHILI OIL

Hot chili oil is red in colour and made by mixing vegetable oil with dried chili peppers. It is a particularly popular condiment in Szechuan cuisine, that is famous for its spicy dishes.

GOCHUGARU

Gochugaru is the Korean equivalent of ground chili pepper, but with slightly coarser texture. It is one of the main ingredients of kimchi and various other Korean dishes.

GOCHUJANG

Gochujang or hot pepper paste is an indispensable household condiment in Korean cooking. It is a fermented spicy paste made from ground red chili peppers, glutinous rice flour, fermented soy beans, malt and salt. Gochujang is great for marinades, stir-fries, soups and stews.

KAFFIR LIME LEAVES
Kaffir lime leaves can be distinguished by their shiny, dark colour and distinct aroma. They are commonly used in some Southeast Asian cuisines to add fragrance, especially in Thai, Indonesian and Cambodian dishes.

KATSUOBOSHI
Katsuoboshi refer to shavings or flakes of dried bonito fish and are an essential ingredient for making dashi stock. They resemble wood shavings with distinct umami flavour. Bonito flakes are also often used as garnish and topping for rice, tofu and vegetables.

KYARABEN
An alternative spelling for "charaben" (character bento).

LEMONGRASS
Lemongrass is a tropical grass with a sweet lemony yet pungent flavour. It is often added to curries, soups and teas and works well in both sweet and savoury dishes.

LOTUS ROOT
Lotus root is known for its beautiful lacy interior and slightly starchy and crunchy texture. To prevent discolouring, it should be blanched in a mixture of water and vinegar. This vinegar mixture also helps to get rid of any harshness in flavour and potential bitter aftertaste.

MAKI SUSHI
Maki sushi or "makizushi" are another name for sushi rolls. Sometimes the term "norimaki" is also used to describe sushi rolls. Maki sushi is made by wrapping cooked vinegared rice along with other ingredients, such us tuna, shrimps and cucumbers, in roasted nori seaweed

MIRIN
Mirin is another name for sweet cooking rice wine and one of the key ingredients in Japanese cooking. It is basically a sweetened sake, albeit with a lower alcohol content. You can substitute mirin with sake that has been sweetened with sugar. The basic ratio of sake to sugar is 3 to 1, but this can be adjusted to your liking.

MISO
Miso is fermented soy bean paste. It is one of the most commonly used Japanese ingredients and is known for its savoury umami flavour. Lighter coloured miso is fermented for a shorter time and has a milder flavour, which makes it great for soups, light sauces and vegetable dishes. The darker varieties are saltier and are usually used for richer and heartier dishes, such as stews and braises.

NORI SEAWEED
Nori seaweed refers to roasted paper-thin seaweed, generally used to roll maki sushi (sushi rolls) and wrap rice balls. Nori seaweed can be shredded into fine strips and used as condiment for many dishes. It is also a very common ingredient for decorating bento boxes. Good quality nori seaweed is glossy and blackish-purple in colour.

OKONOMIYAKI
Another name for okonomiyaki is Japanese savoury pancake or pizza. It consists of batter, cabbage and toppings varying from meat, seafood and vegetables. Once cooked, okonomiyaki is typically served with tonkatsu sauce, mayonnaise, aonori, bonito flakes and pickled ginger.

ONIGIRI
Rice balls typically made with short or medium grain rice. Onigiri should be shaped when the rice is still warm.

OYSTER SAUCE
Oyster sauce is a widely used condiment in Chinese cooking and has a savoury and slightly sweet flavour. Traditionally, oyster sauce is produced by simmering oysters in water until the liquid has thickened. Nowadays, most oyster sauce products are made up of sugar, soy sauce, salt, water, cornstarch, caramel and oyster extract. Some oyster sauce products also contain monosodium glutamate (MSG), especially the cheaper brands. Do some label reading and look for an MSG-free variety.

PAK CHOI
Pak choi is a popular Chinese vegetable, also known as bok choy. Its mild flavour and crisp texture makes it a favoured ingredient for steaming, stir-frying and braising. Chinese (Napa) cabbage can work as a substitute if pak choi is not available at your local Asian grocery store.

PANKO
Panko is Japanese-style bread crumbs. They are coarser in texture which makes them crispier and crunchier than Western-style breadcrumbs when fried.

RICE CAKES
Rice cakes come in different shapes, textures and sizes, depending on where they originate. The rice cakes used in one of the recipes in this book (page 94) are Korean rice cakes or *tteok*. They are made from glutinous rice flour and are typically chewy in texture.

RICE VERMICELLI
Rice Vermicelli are thin rice-based noodles, used primarily in Asian cooking. They are available in various thickness and can be found in most Asian grocery stores.

SAKE
Sake is made from fermented rice. It is the most popular beverage in Japan and a central ingredient in Japanese cooking. Substitute with dry sherry when unavailable.

SAKURA DENBU

Pink and fluffy cod flakes which are often used to decorate various Japanese rice-based dishes. Sakura denbu is made of boiled fish that has been mashed and seasoned with salt, sugar, sake , mirin and a tiny bit of red food colouring.

SAMBAL OELEK

Sambal oelek is a spicy condiment made of raw chili paste and salt. It can be used as a base for making other types of chili paste or to add heat to a dish.

SESAME OIL

Sesame oil is frequently used in East Asian cooking as condiment and flavour enhancer. Made from pressed and roasted sesame seeds, it is very aromatic and works well for marinades, salad dressings and quick stir-frying.

SHAOXING WINE

Shaoxing wine is a type of rice wine which originates from Shaoxing, China. It is widely used in Chinese cooking and is also suitable for drinking. Dry sherry is a good substitute, if Shaoxing wine is not available locally.

SHIBAZUKE

Shibazuke is a traditional Japanese pickle, made of eggplant, cucumber, perilla leaves and plum vinegar. This salty and slightly sour Kyoto specialty has a crisp texture and tastes great when eaten together with rice and bold, meaty dishes. The pickling liquid from shibazuke can also be used to dye peeled boiled eggs blue.

SHICHIMI TOGARASHI

Also known as Japanese 7 Spice Powder, shichimi togarashi is an assortment of seven different ingredients, including ground red chili pepper, dried orange peel, sesame seeds, seaweed, sansho pepper, garlic and hemp seeds. This condiment is often used for sprinkling over udon noodles, soups, tempuras and grilled dishes

SHRIMP PASTE

Shrimp paste is commonly used in Southeast Asian cuisine. It is, for example, known as terasi in Indonesian and Belacan in Malay. Made from fermented ground shrimp and salt, shrimp paste has an intense, pungent aroma. However, when combined with other ingredients, it helps to bring out the flavour of the other ingredients, resulting in a very flavourful dish.

SOY SAUCE

Soy sauce is a common condiment and seasoning in East and Southeast Asian cooking. It is made by fermenting soy beans and roasted wheat in brine, which in the end results in salty, brown liquid. The soy sauce used in the recipes of this book is regular dark soy sauce of Japanese origin.

SUSHI

Vinegared rice combined with other ingredients – typically raw fish and other seafood. However, as sushi is gaining popularity all over the world, various cooked toppings and fillings are widely available. Some examples of popular sushi in the West include shrimp tempura sushi rolls, fried chicken sushi rolls and California sushi rolls, which consist of vinegared rice, imitation crab, avocado and mayonnaise wrapped in nori seaweed.

SWEET SOY SAUCE

Sweet soy sauce or *kecap manis* originates from Indonesia. Like its name, it is sweet and has a syrupy consistency. Sweet soy sauce is a staple ingredient for many Indonesian dishes, such as *sate* (grilled and skewered marinated meat) and *nasi goreng* (fried rice).

TAKOYAKI

Ball-shaped fried dumplings, which originate from Osaka, Japan. Also known as "octopus balls", these dumplings are made of wheat-flour based batter and usually filled with chopped octopus, green onions, tempura scraps and pickled red ginger.

TAKUAN

Takuan is a yellow, cylindrical pickled daikon radish, usually served in slices as a side dish in Japanese cusine. It has a firm, crunchy texture and tangy flavour.

TAMAGOYAKI

Tamagoyaki is Japanese-style rolled omelet. It is typically made with a rectangular tamagoyaki pan and when ready, it looks like a delicate log.

TEMPURA

Tempura is one of the most popular Japanese dishes in the West. It refers to seafood and vegetables that have been dipped in cold batter and then deep-fried.

TERIYAKI

Teriyaki is often misunderstood as the name of a Japanese sauce. It is in fact a Japanese cooking technique which requires broiling or grilling food (usually fish or meat) with sweet glaze marinade. This book uses a non-traditional and quicker method of cooking teriyaki, that involves cooking meat in sweet sauce until a thick glaze is formed.

TOBIKO

Tobiko or flying fish roe is often used to decorate sushi and sprinkled on top of various other Japanese dishes as garnish. Natural tobiko is crunchy in texture and orange in colour. However, tobiko is also sometimes sold in different colours and flavours, such as green (wasabi), black (squid ink), yellow (yuzu citrus) and red (beetroot).

TOFU

Tofu or beancurd in English, is rich in proteins, vitamins and minerals. It is a staple in Asian cuisines and is a very versatile ingredient due to its ability to absorb new flavours. There are two main types of tofu: soft tofu and regular or firm tofu. Soft tofu tastes great when braised with meat and added to soups, while firm tofu is best sautéed or fried.

TONKATSU SAUCE

Tonkatsu sauce is generally served together as a condiment for tonkatsu (Japanese-style deep-fried pork cutlets) and other Japanese deep fried dishes. It is made from a mixture of fruit and vegetable purées and tastes like a thicker and sweeter variant of Worcestershire sauce.

UDON NOODLES

Udon noodles are thick, wheat-based Japanese noodles, commonly served in soups or stir-fried with various ingredients. Usually pre-boiled and sold refrigerated or frozen, they are also available dry. Common toppings for udon noodle soups include prawn or vegetable tempura, kamaboko (Japanese fish cakes) and aburaage (fried tofu).

UMEBOSHI

Umeboshi are unripe plums that have been pickled in brine together with perilla leaves. In Japan, a piece of umeboshi is often included in a bento box on top of rice to symbolise the flag of Japan. It is also believed that umeboshi help fight bacteria and are good for digestion.

WATER SPINACH

Water spinach is a leafy green vegetable that originates from East India. Despite its name, it is not related to regular spinach and has delightfully crispy stems.

WONTONS

Wontons are one of the most well-known Chinese dumplings in the West. They are usually filled with a mixture of pork, shrimps and vegetables and wrapped in a thin dough, made of flour, egg and water. Wontons are typically served boiled in soups or deep fried. Commercially produced wonton wrappers are generally yellow in colour and square in shape.

YUKARI

Yukari is a type of rice sprinkles made from red shiso (perilla) leaves, salt and sugar. It is very popular in Japan and is often mixed with rice to make rice balls or used as garnish for a variety of dishes.

AFTERWORD

This personal cookbook project involved months of hard work and sleepless nights. After all this is my first cookbook ever! The last couple of months I was mainly cooking, photographing, writing, researching about self-publishing, illustrating, proofreading, more researching, pulling my hair out from time to time, finessing my work, changing my cookbook layout for the xxx times, more researching and more pulling my hair out while banging my head against the wall in between.

Exaggeration aside, it was simply mind-boggling to do EVERYTHING myself – I was basically the author, the creative director, the editor, the illustrator, the recipe developer, the food stylist, the photographer and the graphic designer! The degree of complexity and commitment involved in creating a book yourself is overwhelming, and I have a new found respect for other independent authors and self-publishers out there. But the most important thing is, this cookbook is finally completed and I am proud of what I have achieved – at least for the time being.

For somebody who is quite self-critical, I believe there are plenty of rooms for improvement. By the time I am writing this line, a list of things that I should do better next time are already pouring into my head: *I should take a course in photography, I should think of a more efficient and creative book layout, maybe I should even hire a professional editor, I should do more research on printers that produce good quality books but wouldn't make me broke...* and the list goes on. Nonetheless, I think I have created a pretty decent book with the skills that I currently have and I deserve to give myself a pat on the back.

I hope you find this cookbook useful and would enjoy reading every single page of it. If you don't, please don't hate on me, but if you do, send me some love by commenting on my food blog: cookinggallery.blogspot.com or shoot me an e-mail to: cookinggallery@yahoo.de. I would love to hear what you think about this cookbook. Any constructive feedback would also be greatly appreciated! Maybe there would even be a second book!

COOKINGGALLERY@YAHOO.DE

COOKINGGALLERY.BLOGSPOT.COM

FACEBOOK.COM/BENTOGALLERY

PINTEREST.COM/COOKINGGALLERY

INSTAGRAM.COM/COOKINGGALLERY